Broken Hearts
Shattered Trust

Broken Hearts
Shattered Trust

Workplace Abuse of Staff in the Church

Dr. John K. Setser

Brian Riggins
Editor

Jennifer Plamann
Graphic Design

Table of Contents

Introduction 9

Chapter One
Factors that Turn Senior Pastors into Wounding Agents   13
   Personal Developmental Damage   14
   Inflated Ego   16
   A Drive Toward Ministerial Success   19
   Role Stress   22
   Job Stress   25
   System Stress   27
   Burnout   29
   A Conflicted Self   30
   The Ideal Self   31
   Narcissism, Compulsivity, and Depressed Dependency   32

Chapter Two
Toxic Churches   37
   Corporate Mandate vs. Spiritual Paradigm   38
   A Hierarchical Structure   42
   Corporate Expectations   44
   Over-Emphasis on Power   45
   Senior Pastor Dominance   49
   Role Conflict   52
   Why Corporate Mandates Make Churches Toxic   54

Chapter Three
Methods of Indoctrination   57
   Suppression   58
   Assimilation   60
   A Closed System of Logic   64
   Protocol Management   65
   Intimidation   67

Chapter Four
Psychological Coercion 69
    Biderman's Stages 69
    Biderman's Stages in the Church 70
    Denial as a Defensive Tactic 72
    The Effects of Psychological Coercion 73
    Writing off the Abuse 74

Chapter Five
Trust Injuries and their Effects 77
    Dissociative Identity Disorder 78
    Post-Traumatic Stress Disorder 79
    Types of Loss 81
    Material Loss 81
    Relationship Loss 83
    Intrapsychic Loss 85
    Functional Loss 86
    Role Loss 87
    Systemic Loss 87
    The Cumulative Effect of Loss 88
    Reactions to Loss and Grief 89

Chapter Six
Terrible Tales...Hope For Healing 93
    Process Experiences 93
    Encounter Experiences 94
    What Process & Encounter Groups Mean for the Wounded 95
    Brian's Story 96
    Group Discussion 101
    Wendy's Story 105
    Group Discussion 108
    Kevin's Story 109
    Group Discussion 112
    Linda's Story 114
    Group Discussion 114
    Martin's Story 116
    Group Discussion 118
    Eric's Story 119
    Group Discussion 121

Allison's Story   122
Group Discussion   124
Reflections   125
Postscript   127

Chapter Seven
Wisdom in the Midst of Madness   129

Assessing a Leader's Wounding Potential   129
Survival Skills   131
Where to Begin if You've been Wounded   132
If Reconciliation is Your Goal   135
Forgiveness: A Plausible Definition   138
Fulfilling Righteousness   139
Epilogue   141
End Notes   143
Bibliography   155

Introduction

I was twenty-five years old when a kind and godly pastor asked me to be his assistant. Being fresh out of seminary, I was flattered that he even knew my name. I happily accepted his offer and settled into my first church staff position. It was great. The work was fun, people were friendly and the senior pastor was becoming a trusted mentor to me. Best of all, he made me feel like I was part of his family. I remember thinking his wife made the most wonderful chocolate pie on the planet. As my dad used to say, I would have wrestled a herd of turtles for that man.

Part of my job was to interact with congregants, listen to their needs, and provide assistance. I was good at my job and people liked me, which was fine until my popularity caught the notice of the senior pastor. One day out of the blue, he asked me why I was trying to steal the church away from him. I was stunned and told him I would never do such a thing. He listened, but refused to believe me. From that moment on, it was as if I was dead to him. He publicly questioned my character and doubted my calling. I became tentative and watchful. I was careful to say and do only the things I thought would please him. However, instead of approval I received blank looks and a cold shoulder. Finally, I offered my resignation. In response he simply told me that I had made a wise decision.

I was so hurt. In a thousand years I never would have undermined his leadership or authority. I knew the problem was his jealous nature, but somehow I felt at fault. If I had only been more professional, more cautious, or more insightful, maybe the problem would not have occurred. I felt a great sense of loss and confusion. I still miss his wife's chocolate pie.

At the time, I did not realize that I had sustained a trust injury. A trust injury occurs when a person of authority or relational significance in any way harms an individual

9

under his or her care. It is "a violation of power perpetrated by a person with more power over someone who is more vulnerable...it involves a breach of trust, a breaking of boundaries."[1]

The trust injury I experienced was due to senior pastor mistreatment. Senior pastor mistreatment is an encroachment, offense, or violation that causes an associate to experience a psycho-emotional wound. Such an injury can devastate staff associates to the core of their being. A wounded associate's world is broken and impaired. He or she has been harmed by someone trusted to represent God's love and provide care, guidance, and protection.

A friend of mine who had served a large church for many years as a lay leader, decided it was time to embrace ministry as a vocation. With the pastor's encouragement and support, he received Bible training, quit his job and joined the church staff as a full-time assistant. He considered his senior pastor boss to be a close friend, a man he could trust; or so he thought. Soon, something happened that would send him reeling.

Not long after joining the staff, the senior pastor asked him to deliver closing remarks following a guest speaker's sermon. My friend had never done this before. He knew, though, that the senior pastor was aware of this fact, and assumed he would offer assistance if needed. However, when time came, the pastor did not assist him and the closing went badly. Following the service, while there were people still in the auditorium, the senior pastor approached him angrily and rebuked him before all who remained.

For my friend, it was as if a bomb had exploded under him. He felt shell-shocked; unable to think or breathe. After the encounter he slunk away, found an empty room, and sat alone in stunned silence. Before long, another staff member found him and offered an explanation. Apparently, it was the senior pastor's pattern to set associates up to fail, so he could render forceful on-the-spot correction. It seems his intention was to impress upon associates that he alone was the boss.

My friend felt betrayed; traumatized by a leader he both loved and respected. It took a long time for him to recover his inner strength and self-esteem. The incident caused him to be tentative and watchful. He wanted nothing so hurtful to ever happen again.

Sadly, this sort of story is not unique or unusual. A growing number of church staff associates are enduring mistreatment at the hands of their senior pastor bosses. Senior pastor mistreatment occurs when senior pastors, over time or by virtue of one catastrophic event, use power, position, authority, or influence to control, manipulate, or otherwise exploit staff associates. Senior pastor mistreatment is not a leader having a bad day and taking it out on a staff member. It is not being strict, demanding, opinionated, or picky. Senior pastor mistreatment does not occur when he or she corrects mistakes, enforces policy, privately reprimands, or fires a staff employee due to cutbacks or incompetence. The harm of senior pastor mistreatment goes far deeper than just causing inconvenience, discomfort, or disappointment.

Wounded staff associates are left feeling shocked and bewildered. They wonder what could have possessed their senior leader to treat them so abusively. They are mystified by the fact that the mistreatment seemed to be sanctioned by the church itself; an institution considered sacred, trust-worthy, and safe. They have questions concerning what they can do, where they can go, and whom they can trust. But most of all, through the pain, staff associates are confused and angry. They feel abandoned, left to speculate alone about what went wrong in their church.

Chapter One
Factors that Turn Senior Pastors
into Wounding Agents

The vast majority of men and women who seek the position of senior pastor do so out of a desire to help and do good. For the most part, these individuals are intelligent, talented, and compassionate. They would never think of mistreating a member of their staff. However, factors exist which can turn a called, competent, and qualified senior pastor into a wounding agent.

The phenomenon of senior pastor abuse can be traced back to the early 1960s. "In [this] more adventurous period...not only did acting out occur more often, but experimentation within religious systems grew, making the ecclesiastic profession...attractive to narcissists."[2] Wounding senior pastors are not born; they are made. Some are abused as children or have been emotionally damaged by their dysfunctional families. Some give into egotistical thinking and develop wounding habits. Through leadership training, others come to believe that appropriating a ministry vision is the first priority. Sometimes senior pastors act out in destructive ways because they are overburdened by stress, burnout, vocational guilt, or a conflicted sense of self. In such cases narcissistic, compulsive, and depressed dependent tendencies contribute to a senior pastor's tendency to mistreat others. Any one or combination of these factors can compel senior pastors to become wounding agents.

Wounding agents rarely see themselves as needing change; instead, they usually believe that others must change. If wounding agents do not get what they want, they may start acting out in the form of sexual, physical, verbal, or psychological violence. These individuals may be unaware of the damage they are causing. Circumstances that trigger wounding behavior may be as routine as an inability to handle the stress of the moment. Reduction of human

13

conscience allows them to walk right over staff associates without feeling a thing. For staff associates who work under wounding senior pastors, there is nowhere to run and nowhere to hide. Abuse is inevitable.

Personal Developmental Damage

Psychologist Conrad Weiser writes, "Of all the factors that interfere with successful ministry, personal developmental damage is perhaps the most common and most often ignored (or, more accurately, denied)."[3] It is easy to see how this damage can occur. Increasing numbers of individuals are acknowledging childhood abuse, both emotional and physical. This abuse can cause a child to develop intense feelings of "dependency on others and rebellion against them, causing him or her to feel isolated and helpless."[4]

In addition to emotional and physical abuse, significant numbers of adults have been sexually abused as children. For example, in the Catholic Church, it has been reported that boys have been sexually assaulted by priests. Estimates of sexual abuse of girls in family and extended-family settings range as high as twenty to thirty percent of the general population. Leah Coulter, a sexual abuse recovery expert states, "Twenty-seven percent of women (conservatively speaking) have experienced some form of childhood sexual abuse."[5] Such abuse can result in victims losing a personal sense of value and well-being. It can cause their self-esteem, self-reliance, and expressiveness to become warped.

Childhood abuse causes damage that can be both debilitating and long-lasting. According to practical theologian Kara Eckmann Powell, it can injure "the real self and create a profound insecurity."[6] When this occurs, a child can grow into adulthood feeling a deep sense of conflict, emotional imbalance, and frustration. For these adults, self-confidence and peace seem always out of reach. Instead, they are filled with a sense of fear, anxiety, and anger. Because of

14

childhood abuse, upward to thirty percent of the clerical population may be psychologically damaged.[7] Adults damaged through childhood abuse "are seeking to enter religious professions in greater numbers."[8] When these individuals become senior pastors, they have the potential to wound those who work under them. For example, a friend once confided that he had been abused as a young boy. On one occasion his father mistakenly thought he had disrespected his mother. For punishment, his father literally slapped him off his chair. My friend confessed that all too often his staff bore the brunt of his suppressed anger.

Senior pastors who have endured childhood abuse can carry within themselves serious emotional scars. These scars can push them to develop defense mechanisms, which can negatively affect how they relate to staff associates. Three mechanisms are notable: helplessness, hostility, and isolation.[9]

Appearing and acting helpless is a ploy damaged senior pastors use to beguile associates into meeting their needs. On the surface, such behavior can seem benign. However, beneath the façade is an emotionally impoverished individual capable of doing whatever it takes to get what is required. These individuals will maneuver, manipulate, and browbeat if necessary; frequently using shame and blame to facilitate the process.

The defense mechanism of hostility drives damaged senior pastors to move aggressively against associates to get what they need. They are convinced that intimidation, bullying, and coercion will give them this desired result. They gain confidence and strength by controlling people and scripting outcomes.

Damaged leaders who gravitate toward isolation do so either because they do not like people, or because they are uncomfortable relating to them. These detached personalities are afraid of intimacy. They are insensitive and aloof; usually considering themselves to be highly intelligent or unusually spiritual. The needs, hopes, and desires of those who work under them are of little concern. They deny their personal issues, preferring instead to blame others for their problems.

These antisocial mechanisms manifest themselves in different ways. Senior pastors may invite associates to view them as a type of savior or healer. They are not above wounding associates for the purpose of generating such a relationship. For example, a staff associate named Christopher told of a senior pastor who once brought him to tears and then offered to pray for him to feel better. The pain, frustration, and insecurity felt by these senior pastors produces a personality that revolves around the wounded psyche and diverts energy to the maintenance and defense of the psyche at all cost.

Senior pastors who have sustained personal developmental damage are hurting and needy. They require that associates give them the love, attention, and assurance they lack. Their need may take on a frantic nature that pushes them to secure their environment through mistreatment of others. They may not even notice that people are being hurt. What matters to such individuals is that their needs are met and anxieties kept at bay. These senior pastors are desperately afraid that their pain will become obvious to others. To avoid this, "[They] masquerade as rational adults while they cover over a volatile, angry, confused, and frightened core of themselves. Every now and then the core peeks through the mask."[10] When this happens, a tragic transformation occurs; seemingly normal leaders become wounding agents.

Inflated Ego
An inflated ego, or elevated or high-minded opinion of oneself, may also contribute to a senior pastor's tendency to be abusive. Senior pastors with inflated egos consider themselves to be uniquely anointed and blessed by God. They feel that God has called them to a grand purpose. They possess a heightened sense of self and are goal-driven.

"Their entire lives are wrapped around the exhilarating potential released by the acceptance of God's vision for their lives and ministries."[11] These senior pastors possess a strong sense of entitlement. They are self-motivated, deriving their value and purpose from within. They set their sights only on the end result. They tap into their inner reserves and push themselves to create and accomplish. These leaders feel that God has given them permission to control people and manage situations.

A friend of mine named Andy was such a leader. Andy pastored a small church in a rural area. He wanted his church to buy an empty school and turn it into a regional Bible college. His staff was skeptical because the cost seemed prohibitive. Instead of listening, Andy, in the name of fulfilling his vision, publicly rebuked his staff for their lack of faith and mandated that they follow him as he followed God.

Ego-driven senior pastors, like Andy, consider themselves people of destiny. They expect to be obeyed. These individuals believe they have the right to discipline associates who get in the way. Many leadership philosophies support this view. For example, Aubrey Malphurs, chairman of a seminary field education department, tells senior pastors to "deal directly with these vision detractors...if they do not respond, the next step may involve...discipline."[12] Such instruction gives senior pastors the false impression that accomplishing their agenda and meeting their needs is God's top priority. When such "vision fulfillment" takes precedence, mistreating associates can easily be justified as simply the cost of doing business.

Admittedly, not all egotistical senior pastors use their position and status to aggressively promote a personal agenda, but the potential is always present. "[Few] professional groups are more caught up with idealized role expectations of themselves than pastors." [13] The drive to achieve great things may tempt them to view associates as personal attendants hired to expedite a goal-oriented agenda,

17

thus providing fertile ground for abuse. For these leaders, "God's will" can become an excuse to promote self-actualization by whatever means necessary.

Self-actualization, or realizing ones full potential, is often considered to be a legitimate pursuit for senior pastors. But unchecked, self-actualization leads to a feeling of self-importance. Ego-driven senior pastors consider their calling to be more important or "above" the calling of others. [14] For these self-important senior pastors, maintaining an elevated persona can become an end in itself. At its root, such "egocentricity has one main concern: the desire to defend the ego at all costs."[15] Senior pastors who embrace an egocentric worldview can easily sacrifice the needs of associates in the name of promoting their "superior gifts."

Indulging competitive instincts is also a problem for ego-driven senior pastors. As a group, ministers are skilled and gifted people who, more often than not, like to compete and win. During a class lecture at King's College and Seminary on June 23, 2003, ministry consultant Tom Kerns explained, "Ministers enjoy bringing their competitive instincts into every aspect of life, including the ministry." Sometimes striving to "obtain the prize" can be good and even necessary. For example, it is important that leaders do all they can to obey God and seek spiritual maturity. However, it is inappropriate for senior pastors to develop and grow at the expense of staff associates who work under them.

Egocentric senior pastors are not only driven by personal competitiveness; they are also pressured by the competitiveness of others. It is not unusual for supervisors, board members, and church workers to advance their own egos by receiving vicarious gratification through the success of their leader. Senior pastors who are pushed in this way feel obliged to succeed so that such individuals can feel good about themselves. Failure can lead to criticism and even dismissal. Consequently, leaders are tempted to do whatever it takes "to maintain [their] position at all costs...to keep the show going so that [a] sense of…value remains intact."[16] An ego-driven senior pastor's push to succeed and maintain his or her position can come at a heavy cost to staff associates. In the name of pursuing God's will, such an individual can sacrifice values causing an erosion of all that is decent, good, and honest. In short, the leader can become a wounding agent.

A Drive Toward Ministerial Success

All senior pastors desire to be successful. Ministerial success, however, is difficult to gauge. As a result, effectiveness is often evaluated in terms of measurable results such as growth in the size of their budgets, buildings, and membership. If these results are not achieved, their training teaches them that they have only themselves to blame. Church growth expert Peter Wagner states, "There may be exceptions, but the rule appears to be this: If a church is not growing, take a close look at…the pastor."[17]

Not only are senior pastors taught to expect success, they are taught to expect "great" success. George Barna, founder of Barna Research Group, writes that God's leaders "will accomplish something unique, meaningful and special because the Holy Spirit has enabled them…to reach that goal."[18] But what if a church is not experiencing this heavenly reality? Lack of manifest blessing is perceived to be the senior pastor's fault. Barna says that if the church is not succeeding, it is "because they lack a leader who is fully committed to God."[19] Church leaders who are not seeing measurable results are expected to accept shame and reproach from God and fellow leaders as fair treatment for their lack of success. Barna explains, "The visionary pastor weeps gently for… [churches led by unproductive senior pastors], knowing that those bodies are doomed to continued inefficiency and immobility."[20] Under such pressure, it is no wonder that some senior leaders are tempted to seek success at any price. It certainly did not take long for me to buckle.

19

Twelve months after being assigned my pastorate, I was required to give a church progress report detailing what had been accomplished through my ministry. During the year good things happened, but I feared they were not enough. Consequently, I felt obliged to present the facts in a way that ensured the appearance of competence and success. In retrospect, I had been preparing for such a compromise the moment I filled out my first denominational report. Each month my district office required that I list number of conversions, members, attendees, and the like. To my knowledge I never lied, but I stretched the truth as far as I could. I did this because I did not want to appear a failure. Many divisional colleagues had similar fears. We all pastored in rural areas and the joke among us was whether church ministry could include those with four legs as well as two.

Senior pastors are taught that to be successful, they alone must grasp God's vision for the church's ministry. Receiving this vision is not considered a committee process. Barna says, "Vision is not the result of consensus; it should result in consensus."[21] Because of this idea, many senior pastors have a tendency to consider the church's direction their exclusive domain. They expect ministry associates to enthusiastically receive and promote their plans. If an associate is in opposition, his or her loyalty is questioned. Malphurs calls resistant individuals "vision vampires" and "vision vultures," and recommends a process of discipline. [22]

Such teaching invites senior pastors to believe that nothing is more important than their ministerial vision. Consequently, they feel constrained to promote that vision above all else. When a specific outcome or ministerial vision becomes the primary goal, the needs of associates are often minimized. Senior pastors become wounding agents when goals and visions take precedence over the well-being of those who serve.

Senior pastors are also taught to develop a style or strategy that will secure enthusiastic staff support. Motiv-

20

ational speaker John Maxwell explains, "Leadership is influence. Every leader has these two characteristics: (A) he is going somewhere and (B) he is able to persuade others to go with him."[23] Seeking to persuade sounds harmless enough, but such a strategy can become nothing more than an attempt to control others, and that is exactly what some leaders recommend. Barna exhorts, "Realize that the future is not something that just happens; it is a reality that is created by those strong enough to exert control over their environment."[24] Using a style or strategy to control or script a response is manipulative and oppressive. It strips staff associates of their dignity and relegates them to the status of machinery.

For some senior pastors, success is interpreted as gaining individual prominence or notability. However, reaching for personal glory can cause leaders to become jealous when others succeed, especially staff associates. Feelings of jealousy can push senior pastors to take drastic action. Tony Campolo, a nationally-known Christian speaker, once told the story of a woman named Rose who gained a lot of notoriety in her church for the great work she was doing with the youth choir. This greatly angered the pastor, who felt upstaged by Rose. Consequently, he found an excuse to have her removed. [25]

In his writings, the political scientist Machiavelli observed that to promote him or herself an evil political leader might resort to despicable acts. Senior pastors bent on attaining personal glory may resort to the same thing. They may find it necessary for an associate to fail. This goal is easily accomplished by placing unreasonable demands upon the individual or by putting them in compromising positions. Another practice is to keep associates busy with trivial tasks so they cannot accomplish their primary duties. If attempts at sabotage fail, the associate is frequently fired or forced to resign. In these cases, removal is usually accompanied by character assassination. A senior pastor focused on achieving ministerial success or attaining personal glory can become a deadly adversary.

Role Stress

Role stress is the result of senior pastors having to constantly deal with congregational expectations. Such expectations often involve behaving and acting only as the congregation sees fit. I learned about the burden of expectations early in my first pastorate. When I arrived, the majority of members were in their retirement. Although most were healthy and able to get around, many expected me to visit in their homes rather than at church. I enjoyed these house visits immensely. We would eat, watch home movies, and talk about our families. However, as the congregation grew, younger members expected me to be at the church planning, teaching, and counseling. I still made the house visits, but because of time constraints, they were less frequent. One day, to my surprise, a contingent of older members accused me of extending more love to the younger members. Their prime evidence was the decrease in home visitation. This was the first time I realized that these visits were not an option, but an expectation. On the same token, I was sure that cutting back my church schedule would elicit the same response from the younger members. I felt caught between the proverbial rock and a hard place.

In his book *Clergy in the Crossfire*, Donald P. Smith refers to such expectations as role requirements, which he defines as "one or more recurrent or patterned activities of the player...activities that involve corresponding expectations on the part of others."[26] Broadly speaking, I would define a senior pastor's role requirement as a duty assigned as part of his or her function within the church's social structure. Requirements can include displaying patterns of behavior, adopting certain attitudes, and performing various activities. These mandatory functions are often all-encompassing. They "determine the part he/she plays in specific situations or life in general."[27] Senior pastors are under great pressure to fulfill these requirements. They are expected to "occupy particular positions [and] behave in certain ways."[28]

A common senior pastor requirement is that of being a role model. Senior pastors must set an exemplary standard for those they oversee. The constant need to exhibit flawless conduct can be burdensome. In a study of pastors from several denominations, such perfectionism was ranked as one of the top stresses.[29] The need to appear "perfect" also extends to the senior pastor's family. Spouses and children alike are considered role models, causing stress for the entire family.

In addition to being considered a role model, senior pastors are required to help congregants resolve conflicts, and to always do so in a calm and understanding manner. For example, it would be considered "unacceptable for a pastor to express verbal anger at a congregational member."[30] The need to set aside personal feelings and act "Jesus-like" at all times is stressful.

Another stress inducing role requirement is the need to be an accomplished host and platform speaker. At each gathering a senior pastor is expected to function as a master of ceremonies. He or she is required to be informative, uplifting, and enlightening. The success of the meeting is usually considered the senior pastor's primary responsibility. As one leader advised me early in my ministry, "The congregation will forgive a lot, but you must make it happen on Sunday." Furthermore, in many churches it is not enough for senior pastors to be merely professional. Often they must embrace and even cultivate an almost celebrity status. Many feel the pressure to maintain the image of a superstar.[31] This sort of pressure is exhausting because it is unrealistic and impossible to maintain.

Unwavering faith is another role requirement thrust upon leaders. People look up to them as examples of what it means to walk with Christ. Any show of unbelief or uncertainty is often considered intolerable. They are also expected to "live the vision" of their church. It is commonly believed in many church circles that achieving and maintaining this preferred outcome is the way senior pastors acquire respect and earn the blessing of God. Even though a leader's standing before God cannot be acquired or earned, congregants often feel the need to keep track of a leader's successes and failures. If congregants consider their pastors successful, they often interpret this success as evidence that "God is uniquely blessing leaders' lives and ministries, [and consequently] they gain extraordinary credibility in the eyes of their followers and even the general public."[32] However, if the vision fizzles the senior pastor is seen to have lost the Lord's favor. This can result in a senior pastor being ridiculed, disgraced, or removed.

To exhibit ministerial and organizational excellence and be considered effective senior pastors must consistently perform at a high level. They are often expected to be ministerial experts. Today, this is virtually impossible because practitioner roles have been accumulating over the years. Senior pastors are "now expected to simultaneously demonstrate proficiency in motivational preaching, social reform, and administration skills."[33] Add to this a need to grasp computer technology, building codes, and non-profit regulations, and it is easy to see that a senior pastor's responsibilities have grown exponentially.

As a result of role requirements, senior pastors must function a great deal of the time using a role persona. A role persona is the professional mask senior pastors are expected to wear as they fulfill their required duties. Wearing such a mask involves having to act in an affected manner, use appropriate tones, and say only what is expected. Failure to comply always results in a negative consequence. Episcopal priest and Jungian analyst John Sanford writes, "A congregation hands the ministering person a persona, and when he [or she] fails to live up to it there is a definite reaction on the part of many people."[34] Wearing this ministerial mask sometimes necessitates a senior pastor

24

covering up his or her true feelings. This not only requires considerable energy, it is a not-so-subtle push toward hypocrisy. Denying or submerging genuine feelings is something senior pastors are often willing to do; not because they want to, but because it is safer and takes less energy to perform as required than to struggle against what is expected. It is difficult for senior pastors to remove these masks because supervisors, donors, and congregants rarely allow it. Sanford explains, "The collective pressure on us as ministering persons to conform to a persona is…great.[35] Such pressure can effectively force senior pastors to permanently take on their ministerial personae. When this happens, role-playing takes the place of being honest and real.

Role requirements induce stress. In time this stress creates confusion in the soul and impoverishes a leader's inner self. I personally felt so much stress that one night I broke-down while teaching my Wednesday night Bible study. In my case, the congregation rallied around me showing support and offering prayer. Many leaders are not so fortunate. Left unresolved, role stress can be debilitating, and the resulting frustration and anxiety can cause senior pastors to act out and become wounding agents.

Job Stress

For senior pastors, job stress is becoming a serious problem. The never-ending nature of their job is part of what makes it so stressful. A senior pastor's job is never truly finished and there are few breaks in the schedule. Leaders constantly lament their round-the-clock on-call status. Nothing is ever really "done-done."

Senior pastors are expected to deal with problems at a moments notice. This takes considerable energy and draws upon their mental, emotional, and physical reserves. Along with this pressure, they must deal with further depletion caused by a relatively new phenomenon called transitional stress. Transitional stress refers to the fact that "more and more pastors...are attempting to transition the churches under their care from dying to thriving."[36]

One would think that congregants would welcome such a transition, but this is not so. By and large, people dislike change. Consequently, "the more the pastors try to transition a church, the more hostility they experience from their church...and often from the denomination."[37] Hostility puts tremendous stress and pressure on senior pastors and is detrimental to their well-being. Noted theologian Joseph Sittler eloquently states the problem. He writes, "The minister is macerated by pressures emanating from the parish, [and] the general church bodies."[38] This experience of being worn down is hazardous to a senior pastor's physical and mental health.

Senior pastors must also deal with deadlines and time constraints. There always seems to be more work than time allows. As a result, they take less and less time for themselves. A statement like, "I don't see how I can find the extra time to focus on recharging, strategic planning, vision, and personal development when I'm bombarded all day...I feel like I'm being sucked dry" [39] is not unusual. Feeling "sucked dry" by job responsibilities can be debilitating. Senior pastor Greg Asimakoupoulos admits, "Incessant responsibilities...can lead to problems...and even ministry-damaging behavior."[40]

Another job stress is the senior pastor's inability to assess success or personal impact. This can create an urgency to move "in the direction of over commitment and resultant physical and mental exhaustion."[41] Senior pastors frequently overwork themselves attempting to prove they are faithful, committed, and making a difference for Christ. This is why many senior pastors choose to undertake tangible projects like the building or expanding of church facilities. Such projects have a beginning, and more importantly, an end. "[The minister] can stand back and admire the new building and take satisfaction in the completion of such a project."[42]

There is certainly nothing wrong with a building project, unless it becomes the vehicle by which a leader determines the value of his or her ministry. Gauging self-worth by completing a tangible project is a temptation for all senior leaders. However, those who choose such a course never truly find rest. Instead, they find themselves always having to gear up for their next project.

Job stress causes mental, physical, and spiritual depletion. Worse yet, it can lock leaders into an energy-sapping performance-oriented lifestyle. Stress and depletion can cause them to fall into various addictions such as sex, drugs, or alcohol. This happened to a pastor named Danny who served a church of about five-hundred in a large metro-politan area. He had a devoted wife and three wonderful children. I was shocked and saddened when I learned he had been engaging in adulterous relationships with female con-gregants. Danny was always feeling self-induced pressure to perform, produce, and succeed. In retrospect, it is clear to me that job stress was part of what pushed him over the edge. Church consultant and author William Easum warns that today "clergy addiction of one kind or another appears to be at an all-time high."[43] Senior pastors suffering from job stress can reach the point where their ministry becomes destructive. When this occurs, they become wounding agents.

System Stress

Church systems such as committees, programs, and budget processes are meant to aid senior pastors as they endeavor to help congregants grow in Christ. Unfortunately, this is not always the case. Without watchful care, church systems may become self-serving, revolving solely around the maintenance and well-being of the system itself. When this happens, senior pastors become servants of the system. However, serving the system's needs at the expense of serving people can produce what Joseph Sittler calls "vocational guilt." This occurs when a leader, knowing he or

27

she has received a spiritual call, instead ends up managing and protecting systems.

For example, a minister I interviewed named Charles once befriended a student named Thad who formerly had a drug problem. Officials of the school were aware of his past, but accepted him because he had been clean for years. One day, while Charles and another student were riding in Thad's car, Charles saw a vial in the ashtray. Thad explained that it was an old piece of paraphernalia he had used years ago. He kept it as a reminder of what he must never do again.

Despite this explanation, the student riding in the car told school officials what he had seen. The officials decided that even though Thad had not broken any rules, he had to be expelled to protect the school's reputation. Charles stood up for Thad, but to no avail. Later, Charles was warned to keep the incident quiet. He did keep quiet, but he also had to deal with the guilt of not doing more to keep an innocent student from being sacrificed for appearance's sake.

Charles' experience with vocational guilt is not uncommon. Many leaders who are forced to become "system oriented" experience this problem. They find themselves acting in ways that are in conflict with the very theology they affirm. Instead of loving and serving people, they are pressured to become organizationally-minded and process-driven. Instead of focusing on God's kingdom, they are relegated to maintaining physical plants and supporting religious systems. Sometimes, vocational guilt causes a leader to take positive action like rejecting or changing the system. Occasionally, however, feelings of frustration and anger connected with vocational guilt can cause leaders to act out against the very people they are called to serve.

Also problematic is that in system-oriented churches, leaders are deemed successful only if they support the system in tangible ways. Consequently, they are evaluated in terms of their production. Being valued for what one produces is a source of neuroses, and can undermine a leader's overall health and well-being.

When system maintenance becomes the goal, the incongruity between spiritual call and organizational reality produces system stress. Because of system stress, "there have been a…large number of crack-ups of various degrees of severity among the clergy."[44] When a senior pastor experiences a crack-up due to system stress, he or she is at risk of becoming a wounding agent. Also, system stress can build to a point that it produces a debilitating condition called burnout.

Burnout

Burnout is a negative personal response to pressures, expectations, and demands. It makes people feel "flooded" on the inside and generates emotional and physical exhaustion. It also brings on depression, which can cause a cycle that amplifies burnout's effects. Physically, burnout can induce headaches, ulcers, and backaches. It can cause the adrenal glands to push hormones into the system, which makes rest difficult. Psychologically, it can affect behavior patterns and self-image. Relationally, it induces a person to withdraw and become apathetic or anti-social.

Today, the number of senior pastors experiencing burnout is alarming. It is estimated that as many as sixty percent of all pastors may be affected.[45] A study conducted with the help of the Southern Baptist Convention confirmed that burnout is at the root of many medical claims.[46] Also, it concluded that pastors who experience burnout suffer severe feelings of professional inadequacy. Furthermore, an interdenominational study found that burnout contributes to the resignations of a large percentage of pastors.[47]

The effects of burnout make it difficult for senior pastors to relate and interact with staff associates. Powell states, "Burnout causes a decline in sharpness, empathy, sensitivity and compassion. The person often begins treating colleagues…with a growing cynicism."[48] There comes a point in the life of every burned-out senior pastor when

29

something has to give, and when that happens staff associates are at risk. Weiser states, "Church professionals ...diagnosed as suffering from burnout...manifest symptoms of acting out."[49] These symptoms include irritability, impulsiveness, psychosis, emotional volatility, and neurotic behavior. Circumstances triggering this behavior "are often nothing more than an increasing inability to respond to and function in the complexity and stress of day-to-day life."[50] For a burned-out senior pastor, becoming a wounding agent is just a matter of time.

A Conflicted Self

According to Karen Horney, founder of the Association for the Advancement of Psychoanalysis, the real self is the seat of a person's identity, uniqueness, and personality. Unhindered, the real self grows and allows each person to risk, change, and mature. However, many of the contributing factors I have addressed so far such as past hurts, burnout, vocational guilt, and stress can lead to a conflicted self. In this state, "free use of energies is thwarted...self-esteem and self-reliance are undermined, [and] fear is instilled by intimidation and isolation."[51]

A conflicted sense of self compels senior pastors to employ coping strategies that can negatively impact the nature and quality of their relationships. For example, a leader might use suspicion as a coping strategy which can negatively impact their perspective, causing him or her to become fearful of staff associates. Fear can lead to the assumption that an associate is a threat. Also, fear can cause senior pastors to keep associates at arm's length, thereby hindering communication. Coping strategies may lead senior pastors to actually "believe they should attack others before they are themselves attacked."[52] When this occurs, staff associates are in grave danger of being mistreated. Senior pastors and staff associates, like everyone, long to be unconditionally loved and accepted. Sadly, internally-conflicted senior pastors are incapable of giving or receiving such love, and they often become wounding agents.

The Ideal Self

The pain associated with a conflicted sense of self can push senior pastors into a quest to achieve their ideal self. The problem with that reaction is that the ideal self is an unattainable concept; a fantasy that exists only in the mind. A quest to realize the ideal self can create a desire for perfection, "which aims at nothing less than transforming the whole person into the idealized self...achieved through a complex system of shoulds."[53] "Shoulds," that is, internal obligations, can cause senior pastors to be caught up in the ideal self's urge to be all things to all people. It can submerge the need of the real self to be honest. Also, "shoulds" dictated by the ideal self can cause senior pastors to "believe they should be able to control every situation."[54] Senior pastors driven in this way are capable of wounding associates in the name of achieving their ideal self.

The "shoulds" that grow in the minds of conflicted senior pastors in an attempt to achieve their ideal self are often compounded and amplified by the unrealistic expectations of supervisors, ministry boards, and congregants. Under pressure, streams of "shoulds" turn into rivers of anxiety. When this occurs, the quest to achieve the ideal self can become a vital and urgent mission. It may cause inner panic that can produce waves of frustration and anger. Pain of this magnitude can make acting out impossible to resist. Neurotic acting out is especially dangerous to staff associates who serve at the senior pastor's beck and call.

This dangerous situation is made worse if the senior pastor comes to believe that he or she has somehow actually achieved their ideal self. That belief allows the individual to feel justified in accepting and even demanding the praise of others. One leader confides, "They make me into a kind of holy person...it is easy to let them; I like it."[55] As this statement implies, if a senior pastor feels that the ideal self has been realized, it is virtually impossible for the individual not to embrace an inflated ego on some level. This rise in "egocentricity can be so subtle that [a] carefully cultivated humility only adds to [the] image of saintliness."[56] Individuals in this situation can become dangerous. They are capable of excusing abusive personal behavior.

Senior pastors who think they have achieved their ideal self create for themselves a "neurotic solution designed both to alleviate [pain] and...gain a sense of fulfillment."[57] When this occurs, the boundary between perception and reality is lost. Horney writes, "For nothing short of godlike perfection can...satisfy his [or her] pride in the exalted attributes."[58] In this condition, senior pastors often see themselves as filled with heavenly qualities and divine capabilities. Feeling superior to others tempts them to think they posses "unlimited powers and...exalted faculties; he [or she] becomes a hero, a genius...a saint, a god."[59] Such leaders feel entitled to do whatever it takes to maintain their exalted position. If necessary, they will "misuse trusting people; exploit them...and/or manipulate them with excessive demands grounded in spiritual authority."[60]

Narcissism, Compulsivity, and Depressed Dependency

Three types of negative tendencies are most noticeable among senior pastors who suffer from a conflicted sense of self: narcissism, compulsivity, and depressed dependency. These traits especially occur in individuals who are attempting to attain or feel they have attained the ideal self. Think of narcissism as the need to be in control, compulsivity as the need to do something important, and depressed dependency as the need to be attached. For affected senior pastors, these tendencies become powerful urges, which drive them to take what they need, by force, if necessary.

Narcissistic senior pastors have two goals: "to maintain the sense of being exceptional and to charm others around them."[61] Associated with narcissism is the senior

32

pastor's belief that he or she is something special. This sense of being special produces feelings of omnipotence and superiority. Narcissistic senior pastors believe they have no real peers; a false assumption supported by the hierarchical nature of most church organizations. Also, they mistakenly believe that others should meet their needs and make them happy. Such a mindset creates an environment where exploitation and abuse are the norm.

Senior pastor narcissists have an enlarged sense of self-love and self-importance. They manifest a preoccupation with power, success, and the appearance of brilliance. These individuals crave praise, appreciation, and attention. They often choose to lead through force of will and personality. Furthermore, they believe that their leadership position gives them the right to be controlling and demanding. They theorize that if people in general, and staff associates in particular, will only submit to their wishes, good things will happen.

Senior pastor narcissists exploit associates and deal with them severely. Weiser explains, "Narcissists are fickle in friendship, judge others in terms of usefulness, and reject people with bitter criticism, a criticism they always spare themselves."[62] Senior pastor narcissists are unpredictable and prone to wide mood swings. Their relationship with staff associates alternates "between the extremes of over-idealization and devaluation;...lack of empathy; [and] inability to recognize how others feel."[63] Senior pastor narcissists expect staff associates to do what they are told, and they undermine or discipline those who resist. For them, acting as a wounding agent is just part of their job description, because they consider being "on top" their God-given right.

Senior pastors who become compulsive personalities build their self-esteem and find satisfaction through the perception of being busily involved in important work. Their aim is productivity, excellence, and success. Such individuals have lost perspective and can literally work staff associates to death. They value associates only for what they can do, not for who they are. These senior pastors consider the needs and wants of others to be irrelevant. Completing the agenda is life's most important pursuit; the goal must be achieved at all cost. They see nothing wrong with mistreating associates for the sake of that cause. Their consciences remain clear because they are in denial. "Their own perceptual distortions lead them to believe that they are functioning adequately…the religious professional will deny the presence of symptomatic behaviors, even when confronted directly."[64]

Senior pastors who tend toward compulsivity customarily relieve stress and anxiety by acting negatively and coercively toward staff associates. This may involve throwing temper tantrums, making threats, or demanding favors. These leaders "may not even be aware of the chronic level of anxiety they are experiencing."[65] Acting out for such individuals does not just happen once; it becomes an ongoing and consistent pattern of behavior. Other symptoms of compulsive acting out include various kinds of physical, sexual, or psychological violence; chronic negativity, judging, and the undermining or demeaning of others.

Depressed dependency involves an individual feeling a desperate urge to be attached to people. Depressed dependent senior pastors need to be needed. These individuals project the image of being selfless and god-like, but are not above keeping people needy so they can continue to "help them." Depressed dependent senior pastors exercise authority in order to satisfy their needs and medicate personal pain. They have no problem using the pulpit to dominate people and control situations.

Pride and denial keep narcissistic, compulsive, and depressed-dependent senior pastors from seeking help. They consider themselves to be well, but in reality they are emotionally ill. For these tormented individuals, misery is a way of life. They expect others to medicate their pain. At any moment they may become wounding agents, capable of

34

moving against staff associates in harmful and exploitive ways.

Chapter Two
Toxic Churches

A toxic church exists when "doing" becomes more important than "being." In a toxic church, service to God is viewed as keeping church systems functioning, God's blessing is seen as bigger budgets for bigger buildings to accommodate more people, and looking successful replaces love as the key ingredient. In a church like this, the church building is the place where God resides, and ministry success is measured by offerings received and the number of seats filled.

A healing church speaks of Christ residing in people, not in buildings or programs. It encourages participants to be real and genuine, not appearance oriented or performance-driven. As pastor and author Jerry Cook states, "Love means accepting people the way they are for Jesus' sake."[66] When churches emphasize loving, caring, and "being;" staff associates can enjoy being part of a healing organization. However, when they emphasize performance, appearance, and "doing;" associates risk being abused by the organization's wounding dynamics.

On the surface, it is impossible to know if a church functions as a healing or wounding organization. Even internally, the situation can be masked. This puts a prospective staff associate in a vulnerable position. It is only through active involvement that an individual can really discern the true nature of a church organization. If a person looking to work for a healing church joins one that is toxic, he or she is in for a rude awakening.

One young man's experience while interning as a staff associate illustrates this dilemma. He had entered a church leadership program that promised senior pastor mentoring, Bible study, and a closer walk with Jesus, but once on the job, he discovered that his church was not the organization it had appeared to be. Instead of being loved and cared for, he was treated like a slave and expected to facilitate the church's promotional agenda. To his dismay, he realized that he had become indentured to a corporate minded leader intent on developing a growth-oriented organization. He felt betrayed and used. He ended his internship and stopped attending church. He explained that he loved God, but no longer viewed church as a safe place. Given his experience, it is hard to disagree.

Obviously, not all churches are religious machines. Most ministerial organizations genuinely desire to love God and serve people. However, toxic churches that put organizational success above the needs of people do exist and their numbers are growing. Staff associates who work for toxic churches are in danger of being exploited and mistreated. While there is no way to tell from the outside if a church is a toxic place or a place of healing, I believe the factor that most often plays a role in making a church toxic is when that church exchanges their spiritual paradigm for a corporate mandate.

Corporate Mandate vs. Spiritual Paradigm

God is Spirit, and His ways are unsearchable. His blessings, although very real, are not always tangible or even visible because by nature they are spiritual and organic. God's blessings are not to be measured or analyzed, they are meant to be experienced and lived. Churches that forget this in favor of qualifying and quantifying God's blessings ultimately abandon a "spiritual paradigm" in favor of a "corporate mandate" that measures success in terms of ever-increasing assets.

A corporate mandate is appropriate if the goal is measurable success; not so if the goal is to love God and serve people. This is because the aim of a corporate mandate is, above all else, to benefit the organization. Success for these organizations is defined in financial, material, and numeric terms. The feelings, hopes, and needs of people are of little consequence under this mandate. Of prime importance is making sure that the organization survives and thrives.

A church, however, is called to embrace a spiritual paradigm, not a corporate mandate. As disciples of Christ, we are commanded in John 13:34 and 1 John 3:23 to love fellow Christians in the same manner that Christ loves them. Churches are called to exercise faith, trusting God to lead, guide, and provide. They are not to measure, strategize, or lean on human understanding (Prov. 3:5-7). When a church organization becomes preoccupied with such things as promotion, production, and ministry image, it abandons a spiritual paradigm.

Churches do need to be organized. Whenever people come together there must be leadership, rules, and structure. The distinction between a healthy church and one being run under a corporate mandate is that instead of being served, people become slaves to a mindset that puts organizational need above the needs of people. Embracing a corporate mandate elevates the importance of the organization and motivates leaders to depreciate the value of loving God and serving people. Once this occurs, the organization takes on a self-serving mentality; meaning, whatever needs to be done to protect the organization is legitimized and spiritualized.

There are many ways for a corporate mindset to overtake a church. For example, it can happen when the hard work connected with a season of growth causes the church to lose sight of its original purpose. This happened to one church led by a pastor whom we will call Tom. He started the church by espousing such ideals as unconditional love and acceptance. The church's vision statement emphasized joy, community, and commitment to Christ. The church grew because Tom was committed to these ideals. Everything went well until the church became prosperous enough to purchase a building. Once the building was purchased, it became Tom's obsession. Money, remodeling, and filling seats were all he could think about. Subtly, ministry packaging and a promotional agenda became more important than caring for people. Today, the vision statement hangs in the foyer as only a sad reminder of what the church used to be. The promotional agenda still operates as a demonstration of what a church can become.

What happened to Tom and his church is not uncommon. Many churches begin by espousing spiritual and relational goals only to end up embracing a corporate mandate. It can happen slowly and imperceptibly, that in the name of doing "God's work" conscience is violated, integrity breached, or a situation manipulated. Such things happen all the time. For example, on any given Sunday it is not uncommon for senior pastors to garner emotional testimonies that "capitalize on the emotional bonds that…take advantage of people's warm feelings."[67] This is done in the name of leading people to Christ or raising money to continue the church's ministry.

Manipulating emotions for the purpose of scripting a desired response is antithetical to the teachings of Christ. Nevertheless, it is often accepted and justified as being in the best interest of the church. Leaders who use these techniques are blind to the fact that in so doing, they are exchanging a spiritual paradigm for a corporate mandate. For these leaders organizational success may not be the stated goal, but it becomes the goal by default. In this environment, the staff is especially vulnerable because the goals of the organization are set, not by associates, but by the leaders in the power structure.

Sometimes leaders choose to employ a corporate model because they feel that ministry can take place only if such a model is in place. When this occurs, protecting the organization and making sure its needs are addressed becomes an end in itself. Leaders of these organizations accept the fact that at various times individuals may have to be sacrificed for the sake of the organization. They acknowledge the inevitability of people "falling through the cracks."

At times, leaders lapse into embracing a corporate model if they feel the church has attained a certain status or godly reputation. In such cases, the organization itself takes on a blessed or anointed persona. When this happens, keeping the organization going becomes the highest priority. It is equated with doing the work of God. Leaders who oversee these institutions feel duty bound to put the needs of the organization above the needs of people.

Likewise, a corporate model is the design of choice when leaders view ever increasing assets as a sign of God's approval or favor. These leaders become preoccupied with material success. They fear that diminishing assets may indicate God's displeasure and thereby trigger the loss of congregational support. They worry that such an occurrence could ultimately lead to the organization's demise.

Additionally, a corporate model is adopted when leaders feel they must establish and maintain some kind of religious standard. Rules and guidelines are often spelled out in a church covenant which must be reviewed and signed before membership or staff appointment is permitted. It is not uncommon for these leaders to monitor compliance in the name of ensuring congregational unity. Tragically, members and staff associates who fall short are often judged, disciplined, or even excommunicated.

Churches that utilize a corporate model focus on meeting the needs of the organization. Cries for help from needy people are not heard because individual exigency is not considered a priority. Under a corporate mandate, people are wounded by senior pastors who hold organizational interests in higher esteem than the needs of those they serve.

When a spiritual paradigm is exchanged for a corporate mandate, the emphasis of the Gospel changes. This is because instead of expecting inner changes senior pastors look for external results. Suddenly, doctrines like abundant life are redefined to imply affluent living. Scripture ceases to be read relationally and instead is looked upon as some kind of scientific method "if-then" statement. Likewise, the transforming power of Christ is no longer a seed in people that grows, but a procedure that must be practiced. Under a corporate mandate, miracle is replaced by method, being is lost to doing, and a Spirit-filled life gives way to a purpose led program.

Churches that operate from a corporate mandate become toxic because "the organization itself is [the] source of legitimacy that justifies its goals, activities and the pressure that it [applies]."[68] God's will and the needs of people, especially associates, cease being a priority. The focus becomes organizational success, measured in ways that are tangible and palpable.

A Hierarchical Structure

Regardless the form of government -- elder board, majority vote, or denominational placement -- virtually all churches use a hierarchical structure to promote an organizational agenda. This framework puts one person in control and makes him or her responsible for successfully executing and accomplishing the church program. Sittler writes, "The [parish's]...purpose is specified in terms of a 'program'...the minister, like it or not, is the executive officer."[69]

Although it is utilized almost universally, a hierarchical structure is a peculiar model for churches to employ. Such a model gives one person authority over others for the purpose of determining what is organizationally expedient, and requires that the needs of people give way to organizational interests. Secular companies choose this model because advancement of the corporation is the top priority. It is understood that operational control must be placed in the hands of one person. Such a model is appropriate if organizational success is the goal. But it is a strange choice for churches, because churches should value the needs of people above those of the organization.

In a church context, putting one man or woman in charge of expediting an organizational program is workable if all parties embrace a spiritual paradigm that emphasizes loving God and serving people. The understanding that God

42

Himself is the Prime Mover and His actions are accomplished by the Spirit is foundational (Zec. 4:6). Since God's activity is spiritual, it follows that his workings cannot necessarily be quantitatively measured. However, hierarchical structures tend to require this type of measurement to prove that organizational goals are met. When this occurs, a corporate mandate takes hold. A corporate mandate demands that the leader sees to the health of the organization by making sure measurable outcomes are realized. Under a corporate mandate, organizational goals are all-important. They take precedence over the needs of people, especially those who serve.

Hierarchical church organizations are in constant danger of losing their spiritual raison d'etre and becoming toxic. They tend to equate ministry success with producing measurable outcomes. Churches can easily fall under the spell of such an agenda. For example, it is widely held that healthy churches are growing churches. Virtually every church in America believes that numeric growth is God's will and a sign of His blessing. Consequently, the need to see attendance increase is a fact of ministerial life. Campolo concurs, "Rhetoric that numbers are not important may be glibly uttered by senior pastors at staff meetings, but that does not alter the fact that large... groups are pre-requisites to their own images as successes."[70]

Once the door is open for ministerial success to be equated with a measurable outcome, a spiritual paradigm is lost. At that moment, whether the church realizes it or not, the actual blessing of God becomes less important than the perceived blessing of God. The senior pastor's job title, likewise, changes from shepherd and teacher to president and CEO.

Corporate Expectations

In corporately-run churches, expectations are put upon staff associates that are both exacting and punitive. For example, attendance figures are expected to rise in the groups associates lead. Pressure is applied and termination can result if attendance numbers dip below what is deemed acceptable. Even if an associate is "growing" the ministry, he or she can expect to be reprimanded if the leader is forced to deal with a disgruntled member. Protecting congregational harmony is an important corporate expectation. Campolo observes, "Putting out the fires that are set, usually unintentionally, by unsuspecting church workers...can make... senior pastors very nervous...they are aware that such reactions can be troublesome for their preciously guarded ecclesiastical organizations."[71]

A particularly troublesome system expectation requires associates to reflect the appropriate ministry image. Associates must be upbeat, in control, and positive. Having personal difficulties or being "down" is not tolerated for long. This policy forces associates to cover over problems and submerge feelings for appearance's sake. They are not allowed to be themselves or grow at their own pace. On the contrary, they must "look the part" and conform to whatever image is required.

Corporate-minded churches consider staff associates expendable. They are frequently made to bear the blame for system failures. As one youth worker put it, "I learned I must always be ready: Ready to leave and ready to stay."[72] Although scapegoating is quite common, it often takes associates by surprise. For example, a staff associate named Tyrone was shocked when he learned through the grapevine that he was fired because of "all the things that [he] had done wrong."[73] Corporate expectations cause church-place toxicity. Such expectations place associates in a position where they can easily be used and abused.

Over-Emphasis on Power

Senior pastors are commanded to shun power. Jesus said, "The non-Jewish people have men they call rulers. You know that those rulers love to show their power over the people. And their important leaders love to use all their authority. But it should not be that way among you" (Mk. 10:42-43a International Children's Bible). But in corporate-minded church organizations, obsession with tangible success drives senior pastors to exercise power and act in ways that facilitate egotism. Such leaders can become a danger to the staff associates who work under them. Power can lead to corruption and senior pastors who value the exercise of power are often changed progressively. They can ultimately become corrupt, blind, and hard-hearted; namely, a dangerous caricature of their true selves.

Organization is necessary if a church is going to successfully care for people and reach the world for Christ. Organization requires that a system be in place so that church workers can know their responsibilities within the organization, and the more systematized the organization, the more likely that it will achieve its objectives. However, a problem exists in the fact that highly systematized organizations tend to embrace a corporate mandate that values power as a key ingredient. Though a church must be organized to be successful, every person in that organization must be viewed as an equal. In a corporate situation where power is valued, the tendency for senior pastor abuse is not far behind. Sociologist Jerry Bergman concurs, "Bureaucracy and centralization are important for success [but] the combination is especially potent...these same factors have a large potential for serious abuse."[74]

Power-conscious senior pastors who oversee corporate-minded ministry organizations require that staff members maintain the proper "chain of command." In other words, as in the military, staff members are expected to say what the leader is saying and uphold his or her authority no matter what. In corporate-minded churches a pledge of loyalty to the senior leader irrespective of personal opinion or conscience is commonly considered appropriate protocol. J.D. Watson, a youth pastor, sent the following note. "Finally, Pastor I wish to pledge my loyalty and support to you...I also submit myself to your authority and give myself in loyalty to you and your leadership."[75] Where power is valued, unconditional loyalty is required. But when such loyalty is required, suspicion is the natural byproduct.

Suspicion can motivate a leader to exercise control over an associate, which sometimes leads leaders to use harmful tools like humiliating public shows of displeasure. An associate writes, "Sometimes [the leader] would let me know that she was going to share about a mistake I might have made in the week concerning my ministry and use it as an example how not to do something. I felt publicly humiliated on different occasions."[76]

A culture where power is valued and exercised creates a competitive church environment where associates stop focusing on God and start focusing on catching the attention of the power holder. This competition for attention can create jealousy. The successful individual "can become the focus of anger, suspicion and hostility from...other staff whose job performance, for whatever reason, does not appear to be achieving the same level of results."[77] It can tempt an associate to sabotage a colleague in order to gain an edge. All of these reactions and ways of treating people are completely contrary to Christ's teachings.

In the same manner, the drive to compete and succeed can cause senior pastors to manifest obsessive attitudes toward the associates under them. For example, upon discovering that an associate has accepted a position elsewhere, it is not uncommon to hear a senior pastor respond by asking, "how dare you do this to me? Who is this pastor who is trying to steal you away?" [78] Such a response exposes the fact that power-oriented senior pastors often view associates merely as pawns of the organization. Executive presbyter Richard Dresselhaus writes that in such an environment, "Associates fear that any expression of interest in another position will be interpreted as disloyalty."[79] Associates are afraid of being seen as disloyal. They know that the punishment for disloyalty can be swift and severe.

Placing too much value on power fosters relational schisms that are common in today's churches. Worship leader and lecturer Tom McDonald observes, "A chasm lies between pastors and... [associates] in many of our churches. The depth of the relational schism varies, but the pain...is, nonetheless, palpable."[80] Part of the reason for this relational schism is that power in the church is centralized in the hands of the senior pastor. Because of this, associates have virtually no authority of their own and are therefore not able to defend themselves. This makes them prime targets for mistreatment. The extremity of the pain and problems that power struggles have caused is so great that one heartbroken staff worker announcing his resignation explained, "A lot of things have been said, a lot of people have been hurt, many people have been let go...and subsequently banned. It has been painful...[like] a state of civil war."[81]

Psychotherapist and professor of pastoral theology James Poling believes that church leaders are presented with a choice. He writes, "Religious leaders must choose whether to collude...or to be prophetic critics of the way power is distributed and defined."[82] The decision is not an easy one. Churches with corporate mandates require that their leaders produce tangible results, and leaders feel this pressure profoundly. They know their jobs and reputations are at stake. Consequently, senior pastors are not quick to put power in any hands but their own. Moreover, pressure to produce results and value the exercise of power as a means toward this end has increased exponentially because the bar has been raised regarding what is considered successful. Today, the "mega-church" is the standard of excellence for corporate-minded churches.

There is nothing wrong with a church being a mega-church. What is inappropriate is that the mega-church model has, to a large extent, become today's measure of ministerial success. A large, prosperous church is considered by many to be spiritually mature and blessed by God. When spiritual maturity is measured by a church's size, it presents senior pastors with a terrible dilemma. Spiritual growth and maturity are construed as mandates of God. Therefore, if a church's spiritual maturity is defined in terms of growing numbers senior pastors may feel obligated to produce such results, even if this means wounding people in the process. During a lecture at King's College and Seminary on June 23, 2003, Jack Hayford, a noted pastor admitted, "Mega-churches have become the model for so many people... ministers wrestle with size." Using and abusing staff associates in the name of attaining mega-church status is no longer the exception, but the rule. Former seminary dean Bernard Loomer warned of such an eventuality. He predicted that results-oriented senior pastors would have a tendency to "run over or trample on or remain indifferent to those people whom... [they] can safely ignore."[83]

Similarities between secular workplace hostility and the hostility found within corporate-minded church organizations is striking and disturbing. Staff associates who work in power-oriented church environments share the plight of middle managers who hold secular positions. In corporate America and around the world, increased competition and reduced profitability is creating "a culture of internal politicking and deceit...triggering a new and more aggressive wave of...in-fighting."[84] Secular executives under pressure to explain losses are "deliberately scapegoating the most vulnerable members of [the] staff."[85] Conflict of every kind is on the rise in the secular workplace. A survey by the Roffey Park Management Agenda indicates that harassment, bullying, verbal attacks, sexual harassment, and even physical assaults are becoming commonplace.[86] In many workplaces unreasonable put-downs, basic rudeness, stealing credit, and dispensing blame is creating low morale and "is prompting large numbers of staff deliberately to sabotage the efforts of colleagues and managers."[87]

Hostility in the church is made worse by the fact that church organizations usually lack an employee support system. This means that secular workers are often granted rights not afforded church staff employees. For example, secular organizations must follow state and federal workplace regulations. Agencies are available to monitor their compliance. Workers often have unions, human resource departments, and "800" numbers at their disposal. Compared to those resources, church staff employees are virtually unrepresented and unprotected. Lack of oversight allows corporate-minded senior pastors to "interpret their controlling and abusive power as an expression of love that can only be judged by themselves."[88] In such cases even the courts are powerless to help. Because of church and state separation, courts are reluctant to look at contracts made between staff and the church. If a dispute occurs, courts rarely get involved.

Sometimes staff members looking to make things better only make their problems worse. Associates who complain or resist are normally branded as rebellious and disloyal. They are routinely disciplined or terminated. If abuses are reported, they are often not believed because a ministry organization is considered a sacred institution. When this happens, churches become toxic, and staff associates find themselves at the mercy of a powerful senior pastor boss who is "above" them in every respect.

Senior Pastor Dominance

For staff associates, the senior pastor can be an imposing figure and a dominant force. He or she is boss, ministry leader, teacher, and spiritual guide. This individual acts as a father or mother figure, plus a Christ figure. A senior pastor also represents the conscience and conviction of the Holy Spirit. In the church, a senior pastor's word is

49

law. Seminary dean Howard Bixby states, "In the case of the church staff worker…no one competes with the pastor."[89]

A senior pastor's dominance over an associate is reinforced by the belief that he or she is empowered by God to lead and teach with authority. Also, senior pastors are considered to possess a unique understanding of God's ways and purposes. In the church, an associate's ability to function requires the senior leader's approval and blessing. Whatever the job description, a staff associate receives his or her marching orders from the pastor alone. Associate criticism or opposition is considered unacceptable. When it occurs, it is "invariably turned on the individual concerned."[90] In a church staff context, the senior pastor holds the superior position without question.

Senior pastor dominance is all the more imposing because of the fact that staff associates are heavily invested in the work they do. It is their livelihood, calling, passion, source of human relationship, and self-esteem. All of this is in the hands of a boss whose main responsibility in a corporate church setting is to "deliver the goods" by producing tangible results. Staff associates are often afraid of what might happen if they fail to comply with their pastor's demands.

When senior pastors transition into a new church, they commonly assert their position by instituting a staff that will bend to their will. As the old leader leaves, the replacement's arrival often signals the hiring of a new staff and the termination of the old staff. This can occur with little or no advance notice. One associate lamented, "I also wasn't prepared for the protocol that typically surrounds…transition. I didn't know I was supposed to offer my resignation. I mean, I felt like I'd just arrived."[91]

Senior pastor dominance dictates that an associate's first priority is submission. An associate recounting his experience explained, "Early in our candidating dance he said, 'Son, unless I tell you to do something that is sin, I expect you to do it.'"[92] A submitted associate's chief responsibility is to advance the senior pastor's program by doing whatever he or she cannot do for lack of time or interest. This means that an associate is first and foremost a paid professional "assistant" who does his or her job as directed. For the staff associate, failure to follow a senior pastor directive invariably leads to negative consequences.

Being submitted requires that staff associates confirm the loyalty of their workers. As one youth pastor told his staff, the "team's responsibility is to help…fulfill the senior pastor's vision first. The pastor is the shepherd…it is important to keep this [in mind]… at all times."[93] Pastors that require unquestioning submission make it very difficult for associates to object or oppose their leadership in any way. An associate's words, thoughts, and actions must line up squarely with those of the senior pastor, and if they do not it can result in discipline or retraining.

That's exactly what happened to a youth pastor named Todd. He was asked to explain why some of his youth program graduates were choosing not to attend the adult church service. He explained that the young adults considered the service too formal and structured. The senior pastor disagreed. He felt that Todd was not being hard enough on the kids. He said that the kids needed to have their sin shown to them. When Todd continued to challenge the senior pastor's mindset, he was placed on probation and told to meet regularly with the executive and associate pastors until his attitude improved.

Senior pastor dominance results in staff associates having to promote the senior leader's agenda. Such dominance stifles creativity and constricts the wisdom of God. Matthew 11:19b implies that wisdom is justified by all her children not just senior leaders. But perhaps more important is the fact that senior pastor dominance can lead to the tragic dulling of a staff member's conscience. Theologian Dietrich Bonhoeffer expressed concern about this very occurrence. He thought it was dangerous for those led to transfer their rights to leaders.[94] He was concerned that such a transfer might cause followers to unwittingly become complicit in a leader's error or falsehood. Senior pastor dominance is dangerous because, for better or worse, it mandates that associates submit and become "one" with the leader's vision and expectations. If the vision is resisted or if expectations are not met, their dominant position gives senior pastors the authority to lead associates down a path marked by coercion and mistreatment. Such action is considered permissible because it is accompanied "by an absolute belief in the rightness of...[the] institution or system."[95]

Role Conflict

Role conflict is the coming together of two or more sets of responsibilities in such a way that obedience to one makes compliance with the other impossible. Staff associates are often "caught in the middle between two sets of people who desire different things from them."[96] Pressure comes on one side from the senior pastor who compels the associate to embrace his or her agenda. On the other side are church workers and congregants who expect the associate to do the same for them, even if their respective plans are incompatible.

Role conflict occurs when role senders expect an associate to perform conflicting tasks. For example, on one hand, associates must organize meetings and promote programs in a way that expedites the senior pastor's ministry. On the other hand, congregants and church workers alike expect associates to facilitate their strategies, even if they conflict with those of the pastor.

A Youth pastor named Ross experienced this problem up close and personal. His senior pastor e-mailed Ross and told him to conclude an upcoming youth retreat with a baptism in the lake. That same afternoon, two youth workers were adamant that the retreat should conclude with a concert. Shortly thereafter, a parent communicated that God told her the retreat should end with a worship service.

Situations such as these put associates in a difficult position. Since they have no real authority of their own, they must try to be all things to all people. This forces staff associates to walk a precarious ministry tightrope. Part of the difficulty is the fact that senior pastors generally view associates as assistants hired to facilitate their ministry, while congregants often see them as friends with the authority to make an organizational difference. The situation is further complicated by the fact that associates are routinely asked to communicate with congregants from the senior pastor's perspective and not their own. This can force associates to speak and act contrary to their personal beliefs. When this happens, integrity is compromised.

It might sound odd for an associate to compromise him or herself in such a way, but imagine for a moment how the dynamic of a weekly staff meeting could put them into such a position. For example, congregants constantly communicate things in private to associates about the ministry or the senior pastor expecting confidentiality. But it is common for senior pastors to require that associates monitor the life and behavior of members "for any signs of rebelliousness or disloyalty."[97] As a result, associates are often required at the weekly staff meeting to report what they have seen and heard. This is justified under the guise of protecting the ministry. When situations like this arise, associates experience an ethical dilemma. They must weigh loyalty to the senior pastor against a member's expectation of confidentiality. This puts them in an untenable position.

Staff associates also experience role conflict when the needs of spouse and family conflict with the senior pastor's expectations. Senior pastors frequently expect associates to work long hours. As a result, time is taken away from the family and relational needs go unmet. Staff associates are torn between fulfilling ministerial expectations and meeting family obligations. Additionally, associates usually work for low pay. However, if they consider taking on extra part-time work, they risk giving the impression that they are faithless, greedy, or disloyal. Such role conflict weighs heavily upon associates. Many choose to quit rather than risk their husbands, wives, and families.

Role conflict can cause associates to deny or lose sight of their ministry calling. This occurs when the pastor's sense of God's will conflicts with what the associate feels is God's will for his or her life. Anne, a ministry leader, felt that God was calling her to start a downtown urban ministry. She submitted her idea to the senior pastor, but he forbade it. He believed the staff should focus solely on his God-given vision. This presented Anne with a dilemma. She wanted to follow her pastor's vision. However, she felt that what was on her heart might very possibly be the will of God. Having to choose between the senior pastor's voice and the voice of God is the worst kind of role conflict.

Why Corporate Mandates Make Churches Toxic

When a person accepts the job of staff associate, he or she comes to the position expecting to be valued and treated with respect. Such an expectation stems from the fact that churches claim God's love to be the center of their belief system. It is also derived from the understanding that a vital aspect of emotional and spiritual maturation "is the constantly deepening presence in an individual of authentic self-respect and self-love."[98] Consequently, staff employees count on their work environment being physically, emotionally, and psychologically safe. In like manner, they expect staff relations to be open and honest, undergirded by a senior pastor's commitment to look out for their needs and interests. In other words, staff associates expect senior pastors to act in accordance with Christian moral and ethical standards.

In addition to this, staff associates look to be treated as spiritual sons and daughters, because they are "taught to believe that staff is a ministry family."[99] This is reinforced by Scriptures commanding associates to treat their fellow workers as brothers and sisters and to honor senior pastors as

54

they would mothers or fathers (1 Tim. 5:1-2, 17-19). Mark Fisher, quoted in *Today's Parish* magazine concurs, "Although a pastor is not the biological father…his relation …is akin to a family relation."[100] Therefore, staff associates have every right to expect that senior pastors will care for them and protect their interests, so they can grow in Christ and help congregants do likewise. They look forward to Christian values, namely love, being an integral part of their staff experience.

These appropriate expectations are rarely met because a false value system runs through many churches. This false value system abandons a spiritual paradigm in favor of a corporate mandate. Such a mandate mutes God's song of love and replaces it with shouts demanding measurable accomplishment. Under this scenario, the needs and considerations of staff members are pushed aside in favor of meeting organizational goals. Instead of "how are you feeling?" the question to the associate becomes "how many are you running?"

When associates are required to produce measurable results, staff relationships are negatively affected. Performance-oriented striving and aggressive posturing breaks out as associates advance their ministries at the expense of co-workers. Conflict is heightened as individuals compete for limited resources. An assistant pastor named Dan recounted one occasion when the women's growth pastor stormed out of the church office shouting that the men's growth pastor had no right taking the sanctuary away from the women. Competition for resources becomes heated and personal when associates come to understand that measurable results are required. Often the difference between being honored or fired depends on one's ability to get the right number of people to attend the right kind of program.

Armed with a corporate mandate, senior pastor CEOs consider their interests to be more important than the needs and hopes of staff members. "As one pastor stated recently while comparing his position with that of his youth pastor, 'I have sought the greater gift.'"[101] A staff member who resists this philosophy is usually removed. Dresselhaus wrote of one associate who lamented to him, "Little by little he undercut my influence until, finally, I had to move on."[102]

Ministry associates are indeed vulnerable. They join a church staff expecting to find love, acceptance, and a ministry agenda focused on helping people grow in Christ. Under a corporate mandate, they are instead forced to promote the senior pastor's interests and an organizational agenda that values success. Since success is usually determined quantitatively, associates quickly realize that they will be fired if they do not generate tangible results. This kind of thinking produces a toxic environment in the church which causes associates to "turn [themselves] inside out to please the...controller [who] is at the other end...seeking an absolute pay off."[103] This end result fractures legitimate ministry expectations and leaves associates sick at heart. Toxic churches are destructive and breed every kind of abuse.

Chapter Three
Methods of Indoctrination

A toxic church environment can devastate staff associates. But with a corporate-minded senior pastor at the helm, it can become a hellish place filled with foolishness, mayhem, and madness. Such leaders rarely see themselves as harmful and dangerous. They speak of leadership strategies or winning agendas, not of exploitation, manipulation, or abuse. Denial blinds them to the damage they are causing and makes them insensitive to the fact that they are guilty of mistreatment. They blithely move forward, seemingly unaware that they have turned motivation into coercion and training into indoctrination.

The goal of church-place indoctrination is to produce an obedient and submissive staff willing to single-mindedly serve the leader's needs or those of the organization. Pursuing such a course has caused many senior pastors who had been healers to become wounders, willing to "wield power to obtain...compliance whenever and wherever needed."[104] Instead of loving people, these leaders have become wounding agents, using associates "as pawns...to move about on the board of the church program."[105]

Every church has a training program for staff associates. Training programs are often ongoing and can come in many different packages. Warren Blank advocates "enlightened action."[106] George Barna uses the phrase "trickle down effect."[107] John Maxwell in turn speaks of "creating a climate."[108] Whatever terminology is used, a process of training is considered necessary to promote staff unity and effectiveness. Training, however, can easily become indoctrination if staff employees are "unaware that there is an agenda [in place] to control or change them."[109]

The difference between a healthy training program and a program of indoctrination is that indoctrination exposes staff associates to processes that are designed to establish control and induce change that robs them of their ability to make choices. Indoctrination is utilized by results-oriented leaders who value meeting their own needs or attaining organizational success above loving God and serving people. These leaders are not training associates for ministry, they are indoctrinating them to compliantly serve a personal or corporate agenda. There are five processes such individuals use to indoctrinate staff associates: suppression, assimilation, using a closed system of logic, protocol management, and intimidation. [110]

Suppression

The focus of suppression is to get rid of staff associates' old behaviors and attitudes. To accomplish this goal, senior pastors adopt an authoritarian style of leadership. They set themselves up as determiners of the organization's rules, policies, and doctrines. They become the group's sole decision maker and spokesperson. They also design and implement the indoctrination program, which among other things, seeks to eliminate past notions and codes of conduct.

To establish control, these leaders create an aura of holiness around their office. They claim that God speaks through them, and has given them permission to act as the associate's confirming voice. They solidify their position by asking in effect, "who will question God's chosen leader?" Authoritarian senior pastors insist they have the right to tell associates what they must say and believe. For example, ministry associate Michelle Campbell explains that her leader "would tell us in our leaders' meeting how God was sick with our lives...many times I would be instructed on what to say and how to say it." [111]

Suppression is facilitated by teaching a doctrine of submission. This doctrine equates yielding to leaders with obeying God. It establishes a leader's authority as final and makes compliance a mark of humility and spiritual maturity. A doctrine of submission opens the door for senior pastors to threaten those who resist with divine retribution. The line usually goes like this: If you refuse to submit, "the blessing of God will be lifted from your life, and you will miss God's will."[112] A submission mandate reinforced by the threat of divine retribution creates an environment where former thoughts about right and wrong become submerged and prior ideas become irrelevant. Staff associates are forced to accept the senior pastor's view of truth versus error and who is friend or foe.

Another submission tactic involves establishing legalistic rules for the purpose of scripting perception and regulating conduct. This is accomplished through the use of official proclamations, pulpit messages, and general teachings. These address who people can associate with, where they should live, and what moral standards they should keep. Such rules always involve not saying or doing anything to promote disquiet within the group. If associates resist, Scripture is applied to force the issue. Using Scripture in this way harms associates. As professor of ministry Ray Anderson states, "The pastor who uses biblical texts and ecclesial authority to gain a competitive edge in conflict situations commits spiritual abuse."[113]

Leaders who use these tactics find them to be effective tools because "the process is so spiritualized that [individuals] usually do not realize what is going on."[114] The use of such tactics disrupts an associate's belief system. He or she is forced to evaluate information in light of the leader's carefully prescribed system. Those who question the leader's agenda are labeled unteachable or rebellious. They risk disciplinary action which includes "being publicly ridiculed, shunned, shamed, humiliated, or disfellowshiped."[115] At the end of the suppression process, associates find that old ways of thinking and behaving no longer apply. They discover that a new and confusing reality has been thrust upon them. After the suppression process has been completed, group assimilation can begin.

Assimilation

Group assimilation is the second process used to facilitate indoctrination. Assimilation tactics revolve around the use of rewards and punishments. Good behavior is rewarded, and bad behavior is met with either threat or actual punishment. This method is designed to motivate the associate to accept the leader's program. Subjecting an associate to a system of unrelenting negative and positive reinforcement is manipulative and coercive because it reeducates, reorganizes, and reprograms the person's mind. Assimilation tactics work best in a closed environment strictly regulated, easily supervised, and difficult to leave. A church setting where associates want to please their superior is a perfect fit.

A commonly used assimilation tactic is a technique called love bombing. Love bombing plays to the need of every human being for acceptance. It involves relentless positive feedback aimed at the person who the leader wants to control.[116] Love bombing holds an individual in place, ensuring that he or she will not exit before the assimilation process is complete. Mary's experience is an example of this tactic. As a newcomer to the staff, she was publicly lauded by the senior pastor. He praised her intelligence, experience, and spirituality. Mary appreciated the affirmation, but it proved to be a stumbling block. Soon Mary felt the need to leave, but remained; fearing that leaving would make her seem unappreciative. Spiritual abuse expert Rebecca Hanson explains that this is a common occurrence. "Newcomers are made to feel so special that they don't dare go elsewhere without seeming ungrateful."[117]

Promising divine blessing for obedience is used with great effect. Being "blessed" may involve the expectation of receiving God's favor or some form of financial reward. Whatever is to be received, the idea is that acquiescence will bring good fortune. Jerry Bergman states that leaders commonly achieve their objectives through the "perception that work done for any part of a church organization…is the

Lord's work...and as such will be bountifully rewarded by God."[118]

The threat of "divine disapproval" is also a powerful tool. Campbell states, "On some occasions...Rob would tell us...how God was [disappointed] because we didn't push ...enough visitors to the Sunday service."[119] To punish underachievement or misbehavior, a leader may withhold sacraments. Communion, anointing with oil, and ordination are frequently used as leverage in the hands of a corporate-minded wounding agent. "It is so easy to manipulate by sharing or withholding grace...often a minister will control his people by letting them know he feels that they are unworthy."[120]

Abusers frequently find an associate's vulnerable point and exploit it. Such a tactic is easy to employ. For example, it is not uncommon for young associates unloved by their parents to be told "they now have a new spiritual family complete with leaders who will re-parent them."[121] For emotionally needy associates, the mere threat of their senior pastor's disapproval may be enough to complete their assimilation. Without realizing it, vulnerable associates find themselves caught in a web of deceit. Exploitive leaders may claim to be loving and caring, but their love comes at a high price.

Threatening to change the status quo is another ploy used to facilitate assimilation. The threat may be to exchange job security for insecurity or flexibility for inflexibility. It may involve withholding of love, acceptance, or forgiveness. The promise may be to suspend discipline if compliance is given. The idea behind these changes is that if the associate will only conform, the senior pastor will be more than happy to be accommodating and cordial.

Some leaders actually require that prospective associates sign a "worker's covenant" giving them permission to use harsh disciplinary tactics. "When we signed the...worker's covenant upon joining the organization we agreed to submit to discipline as administered by the duly constituted leadership."[122] For staff worker Barach Gold-stein, discipline involved submitting to fearful words and actions that could erupt at any moment. Goldstein explains, "He was about 38 years old, stood 6'2" and weighed over 300 lbs...most of the time [he] was a gentle man, but at other times he could be like a raging bull. One never knew at what moment he might explode."[123]

Use of hostility to facilitate assimilation is demeaning and debilitating. In situations where a leader is allowed such physical dominance, assimilation is inevitable. It's nothing more than a self-defensive reaction. Barach Gold-stein's story culminated when "[the leader] lined us up, then went down the row and slapped us as hard as he could on the face. He said the fear of being hit was greater than fear of feeling pain."[124]

Although slapping as part of an associate's assimil-ation is rare, tactics like berating, browbeating, or invasive micromanaging are not. Many leaders commonly use such tactics to facilitate assimilation. Goldstein writes, "He would often tell the board of directors what a great staff of loyal people he has...[but] I have seen him make grown men on staff cry like babies because of his words and actions."[125]

Occasionally, senior pastors will give associates conflicting instructions in order to set them up to fail. Once the associate has failed, the senior pastor can use the failure as an excuse to demand compliance. Goldstein continues, "The worst part of the work was that I would often get conflicting verbal instructions...on one day, I was told to put a section of the catalog at the beginning and later told that the section didn't belong there...I was too cowed to speak up."[126]

Other more caustic techniques include silent treat-ment, shunning, or yelling. "He would scream at the staff and storm out. Sometimes he would scream at a particular person in the presence of the group. The subject... was expected to be simply silent and submissive."[127] Senior pastors also may choose to assign unnecessary work, fines, or pay cuts as a way of promoting compliance. "A person who misbehaved would be told to...come into the office... [on his or her] one scheduled day off...and do some otherwise unnecessary task...[also] a person's rank was reduced...usually amounting to several hundred dollars per month."[128] Consistent application of such techniques condition associates to believe that every act of noncompliance will result in a negative consequence.

Another way of facilitating assimilation is to create a culture of blame. This is often accomplished by creating a problem or fostering a misunderstanding and then requiring that the staff associate explain and apologize. At the end of this exercise, the senior pastor offers to forgive in return for acquiescence. For example, Michelle Campbell stated that a coworker came with rumors about her being obsessed with a woman in the church named Laura. She wondered who could be spreading such a rumor. A few days later she received a message that the leader wanted to talk to her. Michelle was convinced that the entire incident had been staged to force her to get with the program.[129]

When these tactics fail, leaders may threaten termination or promise a painful exit. Threats of termination are very effective, "My boss said to me publicly, 'do what I say or you'll be fired.'...it was coercion and I was the pawn."[130] Associates commonly comply rather than face termination. However, capitulation causes them to feel thoroughly vulnerable and trapped. Many associates also comply rather than face the prospect of a painful exit. Director of Foundation Ministries Mike Fehlauer writes, "Each time a staff member left, the senior person did his best to cast a shadow over that person's reputation in the hope that it would destroy any chance of that person succeeding without him someplace else."[131] It is not uncommon for associates to passively conform rather than face such a prospect.

The assimilation process is undergirded by fear. It is hoped that fear will break an associate's will to resist. Broken individuals will not stand against the authority figure. They will do as they are told. Senior pastors who use assimilation tactics commonly deny any wrongdoing. They claim their tactics are designed to help associates serve God. They may actually believe this to be true. In reality, however, the focus of these senior pastors is not God, but a personal or corporate agenda.

A Closed System of Logic

The third process used to indoctrinate ministry associates is the putting forth of a closed system of logic. During this process, the senior leader mandates what is true, reasonable, and valid. Once this system is in place, all information in the church is carefully assessed, filtered, and sanitized to make sure it fits the system. Associates are considered "ministry ready" only when it is determined that they are in full agreement with the leader's assumptions.

For a closed-logic system to work, senior leaders must have the full attention of all concerned and be considered holy and worthy of trust. To accomplish this, leaders hide flaws by projecting their weaknesses and defects on others. In this way, they divert attention away from their issues and surround themselves with an air of invincibility and superiority. This has the effect of making them seem bigger than life. When this occurs, over-awed associates have a tendency to accept the leader's logic without question.

A sign that a closed system of logic is in use takes place when senior pastors consistently insist upon editing or rewriting material originally written by staff members. In the name of promoting excellence or doctrinal purity, information is refined and carefully packaged in order to maintain the system's integrity. Closed-logic indoctrination allows associates "no opportunity to express doubt or offer any kind of contradiction that would bring into question the veracity of the organization."[132] In a closed system, associates are always wrong, the senior pastor and the organization are always right.

Creating a legalistic doctrine that separates those within the group from those on the outside is a related tactic. People on the outside are seen as misguided or evil, while only people aligned with the group are seen as holy and acceptable. This gives the system a righteous feel. The leader pressures an associate until he or she attests to the logic of the system.

Senior pastors who oversee a closed system of logic lock associates into whatever line of thinking suits their purpose. Indeed, they create a "religious elitism [that] allows little room for outside influences."[133] These leaders never listen to the opinions of others. To them, intellectual openness is a form of compromise. Such leaders brush aside critics by saying they "really don't understand what is going on in the ministry anyway."[134] Utilizing a closed system of logic is dehumanizing. It forces associates to become intellectual and spiritual automatons.

Protocol Management

The fourth process of indoctrination is careful management of church protocol. One of the most important purposes of protocol management is to control what is said about the organization and its leader. For example, in many churches if anything contrary or negative is communicated, protocol gives a senior pastor the right to challenge the offending party and take whatever steps are deemed necessary to correct the situation. This commonly involves withdrawing trust and watching the individual closely. Often during this process, flaws are analyzed and documented. After this, the leader confronts the individual and pressure is applied until the employee repents and submits.

Protocol management also allows a leader to establish the expectation that associates finish projects even if they are exhausted. The stress this generates is often overwhelming. Campbell lamented, "Being in leadership was no party. The pressure to perform and produce…was intense."[135] Performance pressure keeps associates focused

65

outward, while exhaustion insures they will have no energy to assess what is happening to them. This keeps production up, resistance down, and compliance a certainty.

Giving associates low pay is a common tactic. One would think that low pay would be an incentive for individuals to find employment elsewhere, but that is not necessarily the case because low pay deprives associates of resources needed to make such a change. If an associate is already tired and busy, having little or no money is a major limitation. Withholding financial resources, therefore, is an effective tool in keeping associates dependent and tied to the organization.

Sometimes, protocol makes a way for senior pastors to grant low-paid associates a monetary incentive for good behavior. Using the promise of a bonus to promote behavior modification is a powerful strategy. One organization took this tactic a step further. Individuals in this organization were "ordered to make out a check to their favorite charity."[136] This money was restored to the employee in the form of a bonus if they were found to be productive and submissive.

Protocol often requires that associates adhere to a strict lifestyle code. Dress, dating, and especially church attendance are tightly monitored and regulated. "Often [individuals] are required or pressured to attend Bible studies five, six, or seven days…[and required] to do evangelism …recording how many hours they spent."[137] The extreme pressure and pace generated by this code frequently forces associates to drop out of school, quit working other jobs, or even end relationships so "God's work" can continue.

Associates are routinely required to work many hours without a break. One staff associate complained of working non-stop for the church from five a.m. to midnight.[138] Working non-stop creates a time management problem for associates, and that gives senior pastors an effective tool to use at their discretion. "For discipline a person would be asked to come in to the office…costing that person his/her one day of private time."[139] For associates who work non-stop, loss of private time is a devastatingly effective ploy.

Additionally, protocol can be used as an excuse to require that leaders be given final say concerning engagement and marriage. Such control puts them in a position to manipulate an associate's future plans and happiness for their own purposes. As one associate commented, leadership "controlled the right of a single [person] to marry, based on their maturity."[140] This kind of control gives leaders leverage over associates whose lack of submission may be seen as proof of immaturity.

Intimidation

The fifth indoctrination process, intimidation, is designed to crush self-worth and esteem by subjecting an individual to various debilitating and debasing acts. The victim begins to feel that he or she does not deserve even the most basic human consideration. Intimidation says to the target, "You do not merit the common, minimum social courtesies...you are less than [I]...I am more than you."[141] Intimidation can take on a vicious and brutal quality that compounds the effect. One terrorized associate explained, "To illustrate a point he was attempting to make [the leader] picked up a wooden chair and smashed it against the floor."[142] Another associate developed emotional problems when the leader flew into a rage over a disagreement. [143]

Sexual aggression is an especially virulent form of intimidation. A growing number of senior pastors are using sexual aggression to facilitate their personal or corporate agenda. In this regard, the Catholic church is not the only organization that is at fault. Protestant churches are also guilty. In her book *Is Nothing Sacred*, Marie M. Fortune tells the story of Kristin Stone. At the time, Kristin was a 21 year old staff member who worked with children for an evangelical church. One day, the senior pastor brought her into his office so they could talk privately. Once inside, the senior pastor disrobed and raped her. As Marie Fortune explains, "Stone had never had sexual intercourse before. This all seemed so unreal. A wave of nausea swept over her. She wanted to cry out; she wanted to run away. But she feared...disapproval...[and] his anger if she tried to leave."[144]

One wonders why intimidated associates do not just quit and flee. There is no easy answer. One explanation is the loyalty staff associates feel to God and the ministry. Senior pastors can exploit this loyalty by applying pressure that makes it hard to leave. Associates may find themselves trapped by a sense of spiritual dedication or emotional codependence on one hand and fear on the other. When this happens their only recourse is to endure "the humiliation of boss abuse in silence, which takes its ultimate toll on their well-being."[145]

Occasionally, benevolence is used as a tool of intimidation. Such "good will" is designed to facilitate dependency and constraint. For example, one senior leader talked about helping an associate make a downpayment on a house. "He said, if we can [help] someone... [have] a home mortgage they would think twice about leaving the ministry."[146] Once indebted to an organization, facing the leader about making a change can be an intimidating prospect.

Even if it is called leadership training, ministry style, or church policy, leaders who seek to indoctrinate staff associates are guilty of mistreating their staff. Such leaders may consider their methods to be gospel strategies, motivational techniques, or winning agendas, but no matter the terminology used, indoctrination processes are damaging and abusive. They harm staff associates who often want nothing more than to love and serve.

Chapter Four
Psychological Coercion

Biderman's Stages

Indoctrination processes are not the only mechanisms used by senior pastors to bully staff associates into fulfilling a personal or corporate agenda. Abusive leaders also use psychological coercion as a tool of compliance. In fact, the techniques used by these leaders are virtually the same as those documented in prisoner of war settings by social scientist Albert Biderman. Generally speaking, Biderman suggests that psychological coercion is a process by which the target's thought and behavior is altered, causing the individual's will to be broken. Psychological coercion ensures compliance by trapping the victim "in a situation in which the stresses are manipulated so as to constantly frustrate this need to behave in a consistent, learned, personal behavior pattern."[147]

Biderman outlines eight stages in his chart of psychological coercion. [148] First is isolation which involves putting victims at ease in order to determine their strengths and weaknesses, to confuse the reality of the situation, instill a false sense of security, and extract as much information as possible. Next is the monopolization of perception, a process in which someone suggests passively that the victim is inferior, but could improve him or herself through inter-action with the victimizer. Often, this monopolization of perception is achieved through an overwhelming show of force. This causes victims to lose confidence and accept the finality of their situation. The monopolization of perception is followed by induced mental and physical exhaustion. Exhaustion ensures that victims will be too weak to resist. Interrogators strengthen their position by threatening punishment. They recount the harm that came to those who have failed to meet expectations in the past. When fear takes hold, it becomes a strong motivating factor.

To promote unpredictability and keep victims off-balance interrogators grant occasional indulgences and offer short respites from their imposed pressure. During these times of lenience, among other things, "the [interrogator] becomes a sympathetic listener."[149] This causes victims to doubt that the psychological coercion they experienced was as bad as they first thought. In the next stage, interrogators demonstrate omnipotence by exercising complete control over the victim's situation. Additionally, they degrade and blame their victims for this escalation, claming they have no recourse but to inflict abusive treatment. Biderman discovered that generally, victims responded by embracing powerlessness and accepting abuse as normal. Powerlessness is cemented and the habit of compliance supported by the enforcing of trivial demands.[150] This pressures and intimidates victims, causing them to lose the will to resist. Once a target's resistance has been broken, compliance is achieved.

Biderman's Stages in the Church

Biderman's work with the use of psychological coercion was documented using prisoners of war and their captors, but the steps that he describes to force compliance seem perfectly tailored to work in the church. At first the senior pastor isolates and spends "quality time" with the associate in order to control the focus of his or her attention. During this time the associate is lavished with praise; made to feel special and needed. The individual responds "positively, experiencing an increase in self-esteem and security."[151] The associate begins to trust and bond with the leader. After trust has been established, the leader begins to assess the associate's vulnerabilities. The leader then begins to gather pertinent information through testimonies and times of personal interaction. Knowledge gained from these encounters is used to "induce the recruit to acknowledge that his/her future well-being depends upon adherence to the group's belief system."[152]

70

Once the isolation stage has been completed, the leader seeks to monopolize the associate by making him or herself appear bigger than life. This is done either by extolling personal ability and achievement or by claiming to champion a great cause. Monopolization overwhelms the associate and focuses the individual's attention on the needs and goals of the leader.

After this monopolization, the instituting of an excessive workload causes associates to become spiritually, mentally, and emotionally exhausted. Exhausted associates are too weak to process their abusive situation or build supportive relationships. At first they may consider their treatment unreasonable. They may even try to resist, but later due to weariness, they will comply. Exhaustion and the lack of a lateral support system causes associates to become dependent upon the senior pastor for assistance. They begin to accept that they cannot navigate the system without the leader's experience, knowledge, and power.

Leaders strengthen their position by instilling fear through the use of threats. For example, associates are told they will be chastised or punished by God if they disobey. Occasionally punitive action is carried out to keep them focused and fearful. They are left unsure as to what the leader may do next. To keep victims off balance, wounding agents offer short respites. During this time they often perform acts of kindness. By doing this, the individual deceptively presents him or herself as a "benevolent authority that can improve that prospect's well-being...the prospect responds positively...to what could be considered placebo."[153] However, these respites only last long enough to give victims a false sense of security.

Following the respite stage, wounding senior pastors demonstrate their authority by taking complete control of the associate's situation. This is often accomplished through the use of public humiliation. A worship leader told me of seeing such a demonstration unfold during a staff meeting. The senior pastor began by making a joke of the associate's tie.

As the leader continued, his joking became personal and vicious. The associate finally broke-down and ran out of the room. Those who remained were stunned and shocked, fearful that one day they might be next.

After demonstrating authority, an excuse is made to label the individual resistant or disobedient, which enables them to claim to have no choice but implementation of corrective discipline and enforcement of trivial demands. This makes associates feel that the mistreatment is "totally his or her responsibility, while his or her doubts and criticisms are...redefined as personal failures."[154] Feelings of rejection, self-condemnation, and alienation overwhelm the associate. He or she feels diminished and disconnected. "The only possible adaptation is fragmentation and compart-mentalization...many clinicians consider [such] dissociation to lie at the heart of...distress and dysfunction."[155] Once an associate's resistance has been broken, compliance is achieved.

Denial as a Defensive Tactic

According to a report by Amnesty International, during the stages of psychological coercion, the interrogator will commonly use denial to confuse the situation and deflect blame onto the victim.[156] In like manner, denial is a tactic used by wounding agents to mask their coercion. Ray, a ministry district overseer, observed this tactic firsthand when he was asked to deal with a senior pastor who used sensual speech and flirtatious behavior to manipulate and control female associates. Reverend Ray confronted the minister directly. The minister, however, vehemently denied any wrongdoing. Instead, he accused his victims of attempting to manipulate him through the use of sex. His denial succeeded in clouding and confusing the situation.

Denial is a devastating defensive tactic because it not only diverts attention away from the perpetrator, but it transfers responsibility to the victim. It creates the impression that the perpetrator is acting legally and has great power. Coercive leaders exploit this perception because it not only allows them to continue, but it also legitimizes their actions.

The Effects of Psychological Coercion

The harmful effects of psychological coercion are beyond question. Psychological coercion distorts an associate's sense of reality and causes acute emotional instability. The individual "begins to experience a lowering of his [or her] breaking point...[developing] a chronic stress-response behavior pattern."[157] The associate no longer knows what to think or how to act. As associates undergo negative changes, they "begin to lose their personal identity and start acting like...robots."[158] Stages of psychological coercion create an environment where intellectual and emotional degeneration is the norm. The associate becomes desperate, believing there to be no way out. He or she is "reduced to self-preservation tactics. Compliance with the requests and expectations seems the most expedient tactic. Once this pattern of compliance is established, it is difficult to break it."[159]

Unfortunately, the use of psychological coercion in the church has become so common that it is accepted as the norm. Senior pastors who use these techniques are quick to deny wrongdoing. They claim their actions to be in the best interest of God and the church—and frequently they believe it. When symptoms like staff associate depression and demoralization occur, they are not acknowledged as church-related. Instead they are blamed on stresses outside the church.

Amnesty International warns that the negative effects of psychological coercion are every bit as harmful as physical torture. Their findings state, "It is generally held that there is a very real distinction between third degree methods, (i.e.) physical assault and fourth degree methods, (i.e.) psychological disorientation. But they are both points on a single...continuum."[160] Psychological coercion

73

replaces personal opinion and individual conscience with a scripted world view. It affects an individual's "customary ways of looking at and dealing with [his or her self]... thereby rendering the [person] susceptible to relatively simple conditioning techniques."[161] After an associate has lost the will to resist, this conditioning can cause him or her to lapse quite easily into a state of rote and mindless compliance.

Ministry leaders who by accident or design, knowingly or unknowingly employ techniques of psychological coercion are guilty of senior pastor mistreatment. They perpetrate upon their staff associates manipulations that disconnect, disempower, and lock them in place.

Writing off the Abuse

Stages of psychological coercion are forms of senior pastor mistreatment that cause staff associates to lose the ability to properly assess and react to their situation. Part of the difficulty is that victimized individuals have a tendency to deny, minimize, rationalize, and intellectualize their mistreatment. They simply cannot bring themselves to believe that something bad is happening to them.

Denial is the most common first response. Associates find it very difficult to accept the fact that their senior pastor is harmful and dangerous. Such denial is a natural reaction. It keeps them from facing something they consider extremely threatening, so much so that they could be incapacitated if they faced it head-on. Because of this, staff associates often dismiss the possibility that they are being mistreated.

Some staff associates minimize their situation by telling themselves that suffering always accompanies ministry. They desperately want to believe that the senior pastor has their best interest at heart. They convince themselves that the mistreatment will somehow not cause damage, but rather build character and perseverance. Minimizing their situation causes them to tolerate, excuse, and even embrace harmful treatment.

Associates have a tendency to rationalize senior pastor mistreatment in the same way children do when abused by a parent. Children make excuses for the parent to the point of blaming themselves. Instinctively, abused children do not want to be in conflict with those they depend upon. Similarly, associates would rather rationalize mistreatment than be in conflict with their senior pastor boss. However, rationalizing traps associates in an environment of basic anxiety.

Abused associates also intellectualize their situation. Some believe they must remain at their posts in the name of doing God's will. Others think to please God, they must put away thoughts of personal safety. Many leaders espouse this doctrine. They teach that the only way to do "great things for God" is to stop thinking about how ministry is going to "impact you personally." All that counts is the Kingdom and one's ability to "suffer hardship as a good soldier of Jesus Christ."[162] Corporate minded wounding agents insist that associates tolerate mistreatment and offer themselves as "living sacrifices" to the corporate agenda.

Many staff associates in the church who have been indoctrinated and psychologically coerced become compliant automatons, programmed to single-mindedly serve their leader's needs or the corporate agenda. Without their knowledge, they have been exposed to strategies, tactics, and techniques that are comparable to forms of torture. Affected individuals come to believe that senior pastor mistreatment is acceptable, even spiritual. They are locked in place by fear, intimidation, and harmful processes that leave scars on the spirit and psyche.

Chapter Five
Trust Injuries and their Effects

A Christian community is a group of people who interact together around the person of Jesus Christ and the shared norms, interests, and goals of the Bible. Community is important because it creates an environment in which individuals can give and receive love, support, and companionship. Community also promotes attachment, which helps a person "sort out what he/she perceives, think logically, develop a conscience, become self reliant [and] cope with stress."[163]

Building a Christian community requires a radical kind of relational matrix based upon agapé love. Agapé love is God's unique unyielding love. Strong's Concordance refers to it as a "feast of charity."[164] This kind of love is affirming and unselfish. It values people for who they are, not for what they can do. Agapé love is a gift from God that is meant to be freely received and given to others (Gal. 5:22-25). It insists that individuals keep on loving each other as Jesus loves. Agapé love in action allows people to see the face of God (Jn. 13:34-35).

In a church staff context, it is up to the senior pastor to ensure that this relational matrix is given top priority. Failure to do so can cause love and unity to be replaced by schism and dehumanization that may lead to mistreatment. Indeed, the well-being of the staff community hinges upon a senior pastor's ability to extend agapé love to each individual and the staff as a whole.

Extending agapé love requires that senior pastors care for their associates and value their needs. When the interests of the senior pastor or those of the organization take top priority, those who serve are at risk of being marginalized or mistreated. Mistreatment at the hands of a senior leader cuts deeply, causing great emotional pain and even psychological damage.

The types of injuries caused by mistreatment in a church setting can all be grouped under the name "trust injuries." Trust injuries traumatize victims in ways both great and small. In their book *Overcoming Grief and Trauma,* pastoral counselors Mel Lawrenz and Daniel Green define trauma as "the experience of something shocking happening to someone physically or psychologically that …affects the person's ability to function in normal ways."[165] By this definition, staff associates who have sustained a trust injury due to senior pastor mistreatment have all been traumatized. As a result, many of them manifest symptoms that are associated with both Dissociative Identity Disorder (DID) and Post Traumatic Stress Disorder (PTSD).

Dissociative Identity Disorder

The fundamental characteristic of Dissociative Identity Disorder (DID) is "the presence of two or more distinct identities [and]…a failure to integrate various aspects of identity, memory and consciousness."[166] Indeed, staff associates who have been injured by their spiritual caregiver /senior pastor boss experience this dilemma. They are caught between the sense of being painfully mistreated and the need to be in harmony with their spiritual authority figure. These staff associates experience internal discord over the fact that their spiritual caregiver is also the source of their pain. They cannot reconcile being valued and loved by God on one hand only to be minimized and abusively treated by God's representative on the other. Failure to integrate these various aspects causes them to experience an agonizing and conflicting reality.

When any person lives in such a conflicting reality, he or she is forced to adopt a disorganized and disoriented attachment style. "The natural, innate protective mechanism of turning to people to whom you are attached for safety is turned on its head. Your persecutors become the same ones you turn to for relief."[167] For staff associates, trauma, insecurity, and emotional distress results when a senior

78

pastor is both protector and persecutor. It forces the individual to live in a state that Leah Coulter calls "frozen watchfulness," in which they continually ask themselves, "Am I safe?" or "Should I hide?" Coulter explains, "Frozen watchfulness is an adaptation to unpredictable behavior by a loving [individual] who without provocation, is transformed into an angry, abusing [person] and then back...again."[168] Frozen watchfulness indicates the presence of inner panic. It shatters an associate's self-confidence and disrupts every aspect of life. The words "wounding" and "senior pastor" were never meant to be used together. However, this is precisely the persecuted staff associate's dilemma.

To deal with the situation, staff associates are often willing to absorb mistreatment and accept blame rather than believe their senior pastor is unjust. This response generates spiritual and psychological confusion. It distorts an individual's perception of God, lowers one's self-esteem, and invites self-condemnation. It also creates an identity crisis. One moment the associate is "good" because the leader is pleased. The next moment wounding treatment makes the associate feel that he or she is "bad."

Wounded associates who experience symptoms of DID are unable to integrate or make sense of their pain-filled reality. They feel guilty and at fault. Because of this, they often suffer "intrapsychic losses because [they have] lost an emotionally important image of [their] self. Such trauma damages the basic structures of the self."[169]

Post-Traumatic Stress Disorder

Staff associates who have sustained a trust injury at the hands of a senior leader also experience the symptoms of Post-Traumatic Stress Disorder (PTSD). The essential element of Post-Traumatic Stress Disorder is the recurring of "characteristic symptoms following exposure to extreme traumatic stressor involving direct personal experience."[170] Associates frequently suffer such a stressor when they are indoctrinated and psychologically coerced. Leaders who do this are guilty of taking staff associates "hostage" and subjecting them to techniques that modify thought and behavior. Staff members treated in this manner are kept behind invisible bars of submission and loyalty to leadership. These bars are locked in place by the senior pastor's claim to be anointed and called by God. Fear, intimidation, and threats of divine judgment make escape difficult. Mistreatment perpetrated upon staff associates by senior pastor bosses creates a trust injury that causes them to be emotionally and psychologically torn.

Staff associates suffering from PTSD experience intense recurring feelings of anxiety, helplessness, and despair. Other symptoms include "hyper-arousal, which keeps the victim always on guard and in a constant state of hyper-vigilance; intrusion, which causes the victim to experience flashbacks and traumatic nightmares."[171] Hyper-arousal and hyper-vigilance cause victimized associates to become focused on the one who is causing the pain. The wounding leader's position and authority makes resistance difficult. Impotency leaves associates feeling constricted and minimized. Interaction with God and others diminishes as victims become preoccupied with their pain-filled reality.

The tendency to emotionally withdraw and internalize their pain is a dangerous side effect of PTSD. Wounded individuals are emotionally shaken. They often lack the energy or are too afraid to come out from hiding. They do not realize that they are living in a self-protective bubble. Staff associates who choose to isolate themselves in this way all too often embrace addictive behavior as a means of medicating their pain. Such behavior, however, only makes matters worse.

The emotional and psychological anguish connected with a trust injury can cause associates to stop growing emotionally and relationally. Their state of mind and identity become "a proverbial house of cards that will fall upon itself when...pushed."[172] In part, this is because affected individuals have difficulty living in the moment. The pain and rage associated with being betrayed forces them into developing "scripts [that] lead...to bondage to the past."[173] With their eyes continually looking into the rear view mirror, it is no wonder that many associates crash and burn personally and relationally.

Also tragic are the spiritual repercussions of a trust injury. Afflicted individuals find it difficult to believe in God. They feel like spiritual exiles not knowing where to turn. Faith and hope for the future disappear into thin air. They are left feeling frustrated, angry, and confused. The joy of their salvation seems lost forever.

Types of Loss

Symptoms of DID and PTSD are not the only torments staff associates experience because of trust injuries. More often than not, they also have to endure the loss and grief connected with being fired or forced to resign. Wrongfully-terminated staff associates experience grievous losses. Each loss is a blow that causes pain and diminishes quality of life. In their book, *All our Losses All our Griefs,* Kenneth Mitchell and Herbert Anderson provide a lens through which wrongful termination in the ministry can be viewed and studied. The six types of loss they address are material loss, the loss of relationships, intrapsychic loss, functional loss, role loss, and systemic loss. Experiencing just one of these losses can be devastating. Enduring all six, especially over a short time period, can be truly catastrophic—and that is exactly what happens to staff associates whose jobs are terminated due to senior pastor mistreatment.

Material Loss

Material loss refers to losing something that is physical and tangible, like an office, work desk, or reference book. It can also involve loss of familiar surroundings. Material loss is especially painful when coupled with the loss of a meaningful relationship. Mitchell and Anderson explain,

81

"Objects with extrinsic value attached to another human being whom we love cause the deepest pain when lost."[174] For example, an associate named Jeff spoke of missing the choir music sheets. They reminded him of the fun he had singing and worshipping. The thought of music sheets also made him frustrated and irate because they brought to mind his unjust termination, and what he lost as a result. Such a reaction is not uncommon. Mitchell and Anderson write, "We should not be surprised when the loss of a valued object generates feelings of rejection and anger."[175] In a similar manner, lost objects also trigger heartache and sadness when they remind us of people from whom we have been separated. This is what happened to an employee named Martee. She enjoyed keeping her office door covered with cartoons. People would stop, look, and laugh. She was gratified and encouraged by the joy her cartoons brought others, but after she lost her job, cartoons became a source of anguish for her.[176]

It may seem foolish for associates to feel this strongly about music sheets or cartoons, but when staff associates are forced to leave a position due to senior pastor mistreatment, they lose all the physical trappings of their job. Things like sheet music and cartoon strips helped connect them to people they loved and acted as relationship catalysts that brought joy and meaning to their lives. Loss of such relationally important items creates a feeling of "emptiness...the sense of being diminished from within."[177] Also, it produces the lonely and helpless feeling of being cut off from what used to be an important part of life.

Loss of income is a type of material loss that fills associates with a unique sense of dread, because money is necessary for a more literal level of security. Every family has bills to pay and obligations to fulfill. When a person loses a job, both courage and faith can be sorely tested. As one gentleman put it, "It's all well and good to talk about being brave, but when...you have a pocketful of college loans due and a kid on the way as I did, all that was left for

82

me was…shattered ego."[178] The pressure of lost income and position can strain a marriage and family. The affected individual can become a bear to live with at home, and conflicts can arise driven by feelings of fear, anger, and dislocation.

Relationship Loss

Relationship loss is "the ending of opportunities to relate oneself to…and otherwise be in the emotional and/or physical presence of a particular other human being."[179] Barbara Milligan, who maintains a spiritual abuse website, views relationship loss as an event that caused her family to grieve not only the loss of relationships with people they cared about, but to grieve the loss of worshipping with them, participating in their lives, and the loss of their dream of enjoying a fulfilling future with their church community.[180] When associates are wrongfully terminated, they are left behind, considered disloyal, and even blamed for leaving. Such individuals are frequently judged and labeled, treated as if they, not the abusive leader or system, are the problem. When this happens, relationships are never the same, and sometimes they are lost forever.

Losing relationships under these circumstances is harrowing. Associates not only experience the pain of leaving, they also experience the pain of being left behind. They feel abandoned, saying in effect, "If you really loved me, you wouldn't let me go."[181] The trauma associates endure is similar to that which occurs following a divorce, which is remarkable, considering that divorce results in one of the most powerful and hurtful loss events any person can endure. Problems of mistreatment in the church are rarely given that kind of weight. As with many victims of divorce, ousted staff members commonly consider themselves at fault, blameworthy, and guilty. As such, the agony felt in terms of leaving and being left is especially painful.

When associates are unjustly rejected by their senior pastor, they not only suffer the loss of that relationship, they

83

also must deal with having been betrayed and left behind by the leader they trusted. They are "particularly hard hit...because they have had to believe that in the church they have found the one safe and important place on the planet."[182] But, as these associates discovered, many church organizations are not safe. Those who pledged support instead mistreated and hurt them. Mistreatment leaves them shocked and speechless. For abused associates, profanity-laced sarcasm often becomes their language of last resort. It seems the only language capable of communicating the intense anger and disappointment felt toward individuals in general and God in particular.

The deepest and most profound relational loss is often the associate's feeling of closeness with God. For a person that has been mistreated in the church, unanswerable questions penetrate the soul. For example, they ask, "If God is in control, why does he allow [this]...perhaps God is impotent and not in control."[183] Such thoughts can cause confusion and anger.

Feeling angry toward God is not unusual, especially for those who have been wounded. Even though such anger is not contrary to faith, it disrupts an individual's emotional, mental, and spiritual equilibrium. Questions and doubts become part of his or her ongoing life experience. This is especially hurtful to associates who trusted God not only as a personal practice but also as a professional matter of course. C.S. Lewis expresses the emotional anguish and spiritual confusion of many terminated associates when he writes about God, lamenting, "Time after time, when He seemed most gracious He was really preparing the next torture."[184] Staff associates wounded "in the line of duty" are left questioning God's character, even His existence.

Relationship loss leaves wounded associates feeling psychologically toxic. Psychological toxicity is a condition where "people feel ill on the inside when feelings and relationships are not in order."[185] This can result in individuals becoming rageaholics. It is not uncommon for

84

expelled associates to experience angry outbursts that come without warning.

Psychological Toxicity (PT) can also be experienced in a physical way. Paul DeBlassie, author of *Toxic Christianity* writes, "Emotional toxins [can] reach such intensity that the body breaks down."[186] At the very least, PT negatively affects the emotions and leaves a person defensive and on edge. Affected associates confess to being touchy, emotional, and mad all the time. This toxicity creates the feeling that life is not worth living. Its effects are intensified by the fact that wounded associates must deal with their pain without the support of people they thought were forever their friends.

Intrapsychic Loss

Intrapsychic loss is a loss that resides solely within the self. It involves forfeiting "what might have been, abandonment of plans for a particular future, [or] the dying of a dream."[187] The forfeited item may be a personal secret, a hope, or aspiration that shaped the associate's identity, life force, or self-concept. Mitchell and Anderson explain that "When we claim to have lost our courage, our faith, or our grip, we are expressing intrapsychic loss."[188] This loss produces confusion, anxiety, and depression. It may take years for a person to process what has happened and be able to articulate exactly what it is that they have lost.

Victims of this type of loss may not be able to articulate what is missing, but they feel it deeply nonetheless. For example, a staff worker named Jim experienced intrapsychic loss when he was forced to leave the church because of his leader's unfair and unfounded accusations. The senior pastor was focused on advancing his ministry agenda. When Jim questioned aspects of the program, the leader accused him of being disloyal and spiritually delinquent. Although unfounded, the charge struck at the very heart of Jim's assurance of salvation. It drove daggers of uncertainty and fear concerning his spiritual security

85

deeper and deeper. He felt like he was sinking in liquid cement. In the past, if Jim was distressed, he would go to his senior pastor for encouragement. Now, however, it was the senior pastor himself who used a calculated and well-placed lie to drive Jim away.

Staff associates are especially susceptible to intrapsychic loss brought on by their senior pastor because their self-image is linked to the pastor's opinion of their usefulness and effectiveness. Sittler explains, "Ordination to the ministry fixes one's identity where one's commitments are."[189] Therefore, when senior pastors wrongfully terminate members of their staff, they rob them of their self-esteem and force them to abandon their dreams, which is the very definition of intrapsychic loss.

Functional Loss

In the medical world, functional loss occurs when an individual can no longer use part of his or her body. A person who loses the use of a limb due to stroke or amputation experiences such a loss. In a spiritual sense, expelled staff associates also experience functional loss. Termination means they can no longer use their spiritual gifts to benefit their church community. Such a loss makes associates feel spiritually useless and impotent. It is as if an important part of who they are has been cut off and thrown away.

Side effects of functional loss in one's spiritual life include an inability to seek God, attend church, or enter into fellowship with others. Mitchell and Anderson tell the story of Linda, who confides, "I can't even pray now…and I cannot attend any church without feeling my stomach knot up…I have no desire to seek Him."[190] Associates terminated by a wounding agent find it difficult to trust any ministry leader or religious organization. It may take years before they feel able to trust again.

Role Loss

Role loss is the loss of one's familiar place in a social system. Role loss is significant because a person's function, self-perception, and mindset are all linked to the role he or she plays. If a person's role disappears, he or she is "literally without a part to play, and may indeed not know the lines."[191] An associate named Doug found himself in this predicament. He explained, "As a teen I felt called to ministry. I saw myself as a minister, trained as a minister, and was ordained as a minister. Also, I was loved as a minister and served as one for over five years. After being terminated by an abusive senior pastor, I was forced to take a secular management job to make a living. This was very confusing. My new title was distribution assistant, but in my mind and heart I was still a minister. I didn't know what to think or how to act."[192]

Systemic Loss

Systemic loss is what associates suffer when senior pastors neglect to maintain high standards of personal professionalism and integrity in the church. Lapses of this kind can tempt senior pastors to manipulate staff associates to get what they want or use them as scapegoats to protect their personal interests. After being used and abused, victimized individuals are typically terminated and often never work for a church again. Competition for ministerial positions and the toll scapegoating and termination take on self-esteem, confidence, and resumé combine to make future ministry employment unlikely.

Sadly, systemic loss is not a new problem, and frequently there is little help available for those who fall victim to it. Staff associates have virtually no advocates who are able or willing to help. Instead of aiding associates, "The church has a long history of using people to meet institutional needs."[193] Even the courts, which are usually a protector of employee rights, "generally do not interfere in the relationship between churches and clergy."[194] Contracts

87

are ineffectual because such agreements between church and staff associates are considered by the courts to be legally non-binding. Judicial non-involvement allows churches to "impose requirements on ministers that would be illegal if required for other employees."[195] Courts embrace this "hands off" approach in the name of respecting the separation between church and state. Their intent may be noble, but the damage is great nonetheless. Church employees in dire need of help and protection are instead allowed to be mistreated and wrongfully fired.

The Cumulative Effect of Loss

Mitchell and Anderson's six loss types represent losses that people may encounter over the course of a lifetime. However, staff associates who have been unjustly terminated or forced to resign by their senior pastor boss have the potential to experience all of these loss types at once. Under these circumstances, the pain of each loss is made worse because of the connection associates have with their senior pastor. The connection is similar to that which exists between a parent and child. Spiritual, emotional, re-lational, and financial resources are managed and dispensed by the senior pastor who also equips, empowers, releases, and evaluates the associate's performance. When this deep symbiotic relationship is punctuated by betrayal and wrong-ful termination, associates experience a trust injury of seismic proportions. Such an injury causes them to suffer a fundamental sense of loss. This experience is devastating and catastrophic to the victim. "It cripples the individual in relationships and in creative enterprises."[196] Such severe loss, in turn, produces a condition of extreme grief.

Mitchell and Anderson define grief as a "bewildering cluster of...emotions arising in response to a significant loss."[197] If this is true, the grief sustained by wrongfully terminated staff associates must be bewildering indeed. They have been mistreated by someone who they were emo-tionally attached to, someone who acted as a spiritual mentor, role model, and trusted employer. The experience of being betrayed by someone close to you, and then having them removed from your life is painful and debilitating.

In the proper context, feeling attached is a good thing. Every person needs to be loved and cared for. As such, "attachment behavior [is] a normal and healthy component of man's instinctive equipment."[198] A healthy church/workplace relationship is supposed to be about loving and being loved, caring and being cared for, serving and being served. However, when senior pastors mistreat and discard their staff associates the result is intense and catastrophic. These associates experience "panic, anxiety, sorrow, and anger in keeping with the intensity of the attachment."[199]

Loss associated with wrongful termination creates grief that in turn produces "shock and shame at the emergence of powerful feelings we didn't know we had."[200] Darker emotions such as rage and despair can pour from grief-stricken associates in ways that are varied and unpredictable. Associates fear that showing these emotions will cause others to think they have become unhinged or crazy, but suppression only leaves them feeling numb. Even if wounded associates sense the onset of these emotions, they have no way to insulate themselves or others from the reactions they produce.

Reactions to Loss and Grief

A common reaction associated with wrongful termination in the church involves searching for the good that was lost. Sometimes this search becomes an obsession. It can even cause affected individuals to return to the place of wounding. In denial, they pretend the wounding never happened. As Barbara Milligan states, "Although John and I left the church...we returned a few months later, because we were unable to find another church that... represented the Kingdom of God."[201] An associate named Jack had a similar experience. Jack visited church after church looking for the love and acceptance he had initially felt from his abusive

89

leader. Finally he returned to the place of wounding, hoping against hope that the good could again be found.

Theologically, searching for the good that was lost is a worthy pursuit. However, for wounded associates such searching can be a form of denial that keeps them from moving forward. Mitchell and Anderson call this kind of denial "time freezing." Time freezing orders an individual's life around past hurts and hinders him or her from looking forward to future possibilities. [202] This makes it hard to embrace God who is continually making things new and working situations together for good. As Romans 8:28a says, "We know that in everything God works for the good of those who love him" (International Children's Bible).

Betrayed and terminated associates need faith to again believe that God is good. However, faith is hard to find when the surrounding belief system has been shattered. Wounded associates are left alone to pick up the pieces of their fractured faith and splintered lives. In so doing, they are forced to deal with a grieving process that never really ends. William Butler Yeats speaks to their pain. He writes, "When I clamber to the heights of sleep, or when I grow excited with wine, suddenly I meet your face."[203]

For ministry associates, being betrayed by a senior pastor or an entire church system is devastating because the staff person "believed him or herself to be in a safe, just, and balanced system,"[204] and had no idea that the senior pastor was capable of such abusive behavior, or that the system would allow it. Associates realize that everyone is human and prone to sinning, but they never thought to view church leaders as "at-risk professionals...who [may be] highly neurotic and cognitively rigid...or insufficiently const-ricted."[205]

Grief-stricken staff associates are made to feel "afraid that the world...will continue to hurt them...that other people...will threaten and even overwhelm them."[206] Their grief is both immediate and ongoing. One heartbroken individual described his new life as an open sore. Another

90

advised that people wounded by abusive leaders and church systems will "experience a variety of emotions: rejection, hurt, anger, humiliation, fear, confusion, bewilderment, and aloneness...[and that] depression may seem to be just around the corner. Words of comfort from your friends may seem like trite clichés. Your intellectual knowledge does not seem to reach your heart."[207]

Healing these wounds can be a long process. Some associates feel like they are not completely healed even ten years after their negative experiences.[208] The long span of time necessary for recovery is due in part to some associates feeling personally responsible for their wounding. They play guilt-laden scripts over and over in their minds. These false subliminal messages complicate the healing process. In fact, the ongoing lies that attach themselves to abuse can be more harmful than the abuse itself.

Wrongfully-terminated staff associates feel broken on the inside. They often leave the church "spiritually bruised and bleeding...hemorrhaging from a sense of betrayal."[209] A wounded associate's pain is multi-layered and multi-dimensional. This is because the injury is made up of inter-related components, each of which carries emotional, spiritual, and psychological consequences. Every conse-quence creates a painful reality that needs to be addressed and healed.

Wrongful termination forces associates to deal with confusion, undeserved feelings of failure, and personal inadequacy. They often find it necessary to seek assistance in working out the difficulties, conflicts, and problems assoc-iated with being betrayed and terminated. For these individuals, finding support is often difficult. Most pro-fessional counselors have little understanding of senior pastor mistreatment and how church systems function, and even less insight into the pain associated with wrongful termination from jobs within the church. Worse than this is the tendency among many counselors to deny that staff mistreatment exists in the first place. Even Christian liturgy ignores the wounded. In his book, *The Other Side of Sin*, Andrew Sung Park laments the fact that Christian worship as well as Christian practice rarely addresses the needs of the victim or the pain associated with being sinned against. [210] Lack of validation leaves terminated associates feeling at fault and isolated.

Another reason associates cannot find help is simply that senior pastors are trusted by the churches they serve. Literature distributed within some churches reflects this policy, stating, "Presbyteries do not, as a matter of course, interfere with staff decisions in congregations. Sessions tend to support incumbent pastors no matter how long or short a time they have served in the institution."[211] The courts support this philosophy by choosing to defer to whatever denominational system is in place.

Church employees who are mistreated by those they trust to represent God experience overwhelming and sometimes even crippling grief. Any employee of a church that operates primarily as a corporation continually runs the risk of being sacrificed on the altar of organizational success. Eddie V. Rentz, a national youth ministries director, eloquently describes what this is doing to the church over time. He states, "There is a boneyard of potential nation-changers who have become so discouraged they have either left the ministry or now hobble along wounded and ineffective."[212] For these staff associates, survival has replaced service and pain has overtaken promise.

CHAPTER SIX
Terrible Tales...Hope For Healing

Process Experiences

Wounded staff associates are loved and cared for by God. He is constantly at work helping them recover from the wounds they have received. One of the most important ways God helps his wounded children is by using process and encounter experiences to expedite recovery. [213] A process experience is a Holy Spirit-directed word, meeting, or circumstance that aids wounded associates in their quest to gain perspective. Process experiences can seem like chance happenings or accidental occurrences. However, in actuality they are planned and directed by God who actively seeks to grant perspective to those in need. Perspective can come by way of a Scripture verse, an internal voice, or even a casual conversation. Such workings seem natural enough, but they are intensely spiritual and wonderfully practical. Process experiences help associates sort out what happened, so they can make sense of their pain and move on.

As an example of this sort of process, look at the story told by Andy, a former associate who had been mistreated and wrongfully terminated by his senior pastor. Weeks after the termination his mind could still not move beyond wondering why the senior pastor had treated him so abusively. It was a mystery that tormented him night and day. One evening, seemingly by chance, Andy met a man who was a long-time friend of the senior pastor. The man told him that years earlier the senior pastor had been terribly hurt by a trusted church member. As a result, from time to time, the senior pastor experienced periods of depression marked by fits of paranoia. This paranoia would often motivate him to make regrettable decisions. After hearing the story, Andy was able to see his former boss in a new light. He thanked God for the experience of talking to this man, because in the process he found perspective.

Encounter Experiences

Encounter experiences are similar to process experiences, but their purpose is to bring healing. Wounded associates feel great pain due to the mistreatment they received. Trust injuries cut deeply and leave agonizing scars. It is the Lord's will to heal associates using means that are both creative and unique. Consequently, wounded associates can look forward to experiencing the love and warmth of Christ at every turn. For wounded associates, there is a "balm in Gilead" that soothes and heals. God often sends sensitive and caring people to apply this healing ointment on His behalf.

Bill and Phyllis are two associates who experienced an encounter experience that led them to be healed. Bill and Phyllis served a large church as a husband and wife youth pastor team. For a time everything was wonderful. The couple's ministry was fruitful, they were expecting a child, and with the senior pastor's approval they bought their first house. However, suddenly and without warning they were abusively fired. They were blamed for doing things they did not do and accused of saying things they did not say. It was rumored that the pastor wanted to fill the position with someone else, but felt he had to discredit the popular couple to make the change seem like their fault. Worse yet, the severance agreement stipulated that the couple would forfeit an amount of money if they were not out of town in a week. This meant they would not be able to properly say goodbye to friends or even sell their home before it was time to leave. Furthermore, because of the short notice, they were forced to move in with Phllis' parents. Out of time and with no prospects in sight, they left town heartbroken and confused.

Bill and Phyllis' encounter experience came ten days after their departure, when two church elders took it upon themselves to seek out the couple. They felt God directing them to offer an apology on behalf of the church. The elders felt horrible about how the couple had been treated. They told Bill and Phyllis that the senior pastor had acted in a wrongful and sinful manner. They pledged to restore the couple's good name and promised to give perspective employers a glowing recommendation. The four individuals wept, hugged, and prayed together. Afterward Bill and Phyllis expressed thanks to God. Because of the encounter, they had experienced His healing touch.

As these stories indicate, it is the Holy Spirit's delight to set up process and encounter experiences for wounded staff associates. With this in mind, it is completely appropriate for wounded associates to actively seek God's aid through trusted people who are willing to assist. Forming process and encounter groups, therefore, can be a great help and blessing. Such groups seek to cooperate with the Holy Spirit as He works to grant perspective and promote healing.

What Process & Encounter Groups Mean for the Wounded

Process and encounter groups give wounded people an opportunity to tell their stories, vent, assess, grieve, and pray. It helps the wounded create a language of pain they can use to give full voice to their complaint. Such groups emphasize being open and honest. For example, one person may be full of praise to God, another weeping, while a third utters a four-letter word to describe the abusive treatment. In process and encounter groups honest expression is encouraged because God loves it when people are real and genuine. He feels the pain of those who have been sinned against. He refreshes and provides forward momentum as they dare to believe Him to be their ever-present help (Ps. 46:1).

In process and encounter groups, the Holy Spirit binds up the hearts of the grieving. He helps them avoid self-pity and self-righteousness. It is God's will for wounded staff associates to rise up from the ashes of senior pastor mistreatment by the power of the Spirit. As God wipes away their tears, He whispers that He will be their strength and vindication (Ps 37:18-19).

What follows are personal testimonies and group discussion of individuals participating in a Process and

Encounter group. Over a ten week period, five former staff associates and two spouses came together to tell their stories and analyze their wounding experiences. I acted as group facilitator and secretary. The record of group discussion comes from my notes and recollections. Names and certain details have been changed to ensure anonymity.

Brian's Story

I was surprised by people, both within our parish and without, who noted something about me that suggested to them a call to ministry. Freshly out of college and in the early stages of growing a business, I thanked them and pushed the thought aside. It took over ten years and much support and encouragement before I could accept the call and begin training.

I began responding to the process with a personal review. My family and I assessed the financial impact. I would have to sell my business. I talked with my pastor. I spoke with the church elders and ministry overseers. Finally, I broached the subject with our extended family and friends. All involved offered support, cautioning us that we would be starting over in a new profession. But still, all were supportive and recognized my need to answer God's call.

Reality set in when we sold our home and business. We uprooted and moved into an apartment one-third the size of the home we had lived in for ten years. We left our friends of long standing and launched into a new adventure. We were excited, trusting God to provide direction and purpose. For the next three years, seventy hours a week, I focused on studies. During this period, family time was tucked into a few hours together at dinnertime and bedtime.

On graduation day I was ordained as a Deacon, and then the placement process began. A senior pastor called soon after and offered me a position. At last, after three full years of seminary, ministry was becoming a reality. I moved my family to the housing provided by the church, and moved my books to my new office. I then had my first official meeting with the senior pastor to flesh out my duties.

The senior pastor produced a written statement saying that no matter what I thought or was told by the lay committee, I was to work under his authority and direction alone. He alone would define the scope of my responsibilities. He then provided me with a contract stating among other things that I was to cut the grass every Thursday, which happened to be my day off. I felt uncomfortable signing the contract. I didn't think ministry required a contract. But, I wanted to affirm my willingness to serve, so I signed it. I told the secretary that I was looking forward to working with my new boss. She replied, "just you wait and see."

My first six months passed with relative ease. I was only an ordained deacon, so I could not yet function as a full pastor. Nevertheless, I carried a full schedule of teaching, home and hospital visitation, as well as midweek Chapel responsibilities. I robed for the two Sunday services and was responsible for the Scripture lessons and corporate prayers. I was used to doing these things as a lay person, so all went smoothly.

However, notably absent was the fellowship and training usually extended to a deacon by the senior pastor. I was given no education or training as to how and why things were done. I wanted to learn and strengthen my skills. Instead, he insisted upon performing most ministry functions himself. All ministry resources were kept under his control. For example, I was given no pastoral or worship information and no pre-marital or adult education guidelines. It was embarrassing and disconcerting to have to learn by trial and error. I was forced to consult my seminary or my network of priest friends to strengthen my skills.

After six months, I was now ready for full ordination with Holy Orders. I would finally be commissioned as an ordained pastor and shepherd. Each candidate was to be presented by one lay person and one member of the clergy. I asked the senior pastor to present me, and he said yes, but his response was rather perfunctory. This was in stark contrast to my wife who got teary-eyed when I asked her to stand beside me. She and the children had invested so much in bringing me to this day.

There were ten candidates for Holy Orders. The cathedral was filled to overflowing. As I walked down the long aisle, I was reminded of the commitment of early Christians who had pledged their faith. I was proud to be joining them. My heart swelled with the thought of performing a sacred duty, to serve the Body of Christ was a great honor. After the service ended, I turned to thank my presenters; the senior pastor, however, had already exited. I wondered what emergency called him away. When I saw him the next day, I asked him about it. He said that after finishing his task of presenting, he didn't need to stay. He followed by saying something I found strange. He said, "you are on your own now."

Ordination meant a great deal to me. I had hoped it would be a bridge between the senior pastor and myself, and that he would welcome me into the brotherhood of pastors. I hoped to be nurtured and encouraged by him. I genuinely looked forward to serving with him as a fellow laborer. My hopes would soon be dashed.

Immediately after my ordination as a full pastor, the senior pastor became cold and distant. Instead of being allowed to do the work of the ministry, I was given menial tasks to perform. He told me that filling the soda machine would be my "altar" and mine alone. I was stunned. As time went by, it became obvious that the senior pastor viewed me as a threat. I was given limited opportunities to celebrate Holy Communion. As for preaching, I was only allowed to speak twice in the months that followed. It was clear that the senior pastor had decided to expose me to a process of humiliation.

Besides the soda machine assignment, he required that I keep a written record of home and hospital visits. Each visit was to be recorded on an individual card which was to be placed on his desk at the end of every day. Once per month these cards were to be reviewed by the church board. I was shocked and flabbergasted at the next monthly meeting when in front of everyone he counted out my cards for all to see. After my slips were presented, he offered his slips to the committee. They were double my amount. He told the committee that he was disappointed in my lack of initiative. I found out later that the senior pastor had padded his list by counting phone calls and chance meetings as "visits." It was clear that the senior pastor intended to systematically make himself look good at my expense.

After a few months of this, I decided to play his game. I again placed my slips on his desk and again he presented the committee with fifty percent more than mine. However, at the right moment I took a whole bunch more out of my pocket and presented them to the committee. I now had thirty percent more cards than he did. He was surprised and angry. It took him little time to retaliate.

After that incident, the senior pastor asked me and a few other staff workers to select the church's Christian education material. After three and a half months and hundreds of hours we chose what we felt was the best curriculum for the church. We unanimously presented our recommendation to the senior pastor. He looked at the recommendation and said, "what if I do not want this?" We were stunned. It was clear to us that his main purpose had not been to find a curriculum, but to remind all of us, especially me, that he was the boss. The whole exercise was designed to showcase his power. We all felt "spanked" by the senior pastor. We also felt rejected and devalued, knowing that our efforts had been a total waste of time and talent. For me, it was a warning not to ever again interfere with his agenda.

After that, my situation deteriorated quickly. Dreams and hopes of serving God's people were systematically being crushed by my abusive boss. It was indeed a sad time. I finally went to the Bishop and told him what was happening. He was shocked, but gave me no support or direction. He told me to go home and "tough it out." I tried to comply but I could not shake the tension and pressure. Where was the joy in doing church work? I felt like the cartoon character in Lil' Abner who walked around with a rain cloud over his head. Praying seemed empty. I was discouraged and frustrated.

My senior pastor seemed all-powerful. I observed on numerous occasions that at meetings and even at meals, he would never sit down. It was as if he had to be above others in every respect. Even when the Bishop was present and seated, he would remain standing, as if he was trying to be in charge of the room. I wondered what I had done to deserve such a hurtful senior pastor boss. Also, I wondered what I had done to my family. I was not the only one being hurt. My family was hurting too. He often took them aside to explain what he expected of them. It was impossible to please him. We were all very depressed. However, we still wondered if the pain was somehow our imagination.

Out of desperation, I unofficially polled my former seminary classmates and those of the graduating class two years prior and two years following. I was curious to see if others were being mistreated. I also networked with six other clergymen who interviewed classmates. We found that wounding experiences were not uncommon. For example, we discovered that many senior pastors have control issues. Furthermore, we learned that it was not uncommon for senior pastors to place severe expectations upon an associate's wife and family. Because of these pressures, most associates with families moved within a year or two. Finding new placement, however, was difficult for them because many senior pastors consider associates seeking a transfer to be disloyal or rebellious.

It had taken many years to get up the courage to sell my business and go back to school. During those school years my family and I sacrificed and dreamed of future days filled with ministry, fellowship, and personal enrichment.

We all felt the call of God and together we chose to respond. We sacrificed financially, and family time was scarce, but we believed it would be worth while. Seminary training encouraged us to believe that full-time ministry was a noble vocation filled with purpose, fellowship, and fulfillment. On graduation day, our confidence was high.

However, our joy and confidence was short lived. Our senior pastor broke our hearts and stole our joy. He scolded my kids and burdened my wife with unreasonable standards and expectations. I yearned to learn from him and partner with him. Instead, he viewed me as a threat. He crushed, dismissed, and demeaned my every success. He set me up to fail and embarrassed me before my peers. He withheld ministry resources and training so I would seem incompetent. Finally, he cancelled my contract and sent me away with an undeserved black mark on my record. This mark will always be with me.

No words can fully convey the depths of my pain and disappointment. What did I do to deserve this treatment? What did my family do to be treated so shamefully? Our senior pastor wounded us. I doubt we will ever fully recover.

Group Discussion
After his testimony, Brian continued to sit rigidly in his chair. He had recounted the facts of his wounding experience and communicated his pain clinically, but it was clear he had never given himself permission to feel or release the pain. It seemed like he was a volcano ready to spew forth rivers of molten agony. The group communicated this to him and asked if he wanted to let the pain out. He told us that it was hard for him to display emotion. He was afraid that once the pain surfaced control would be lost. Instead, he requested prayer that God would help him release the anger and pain at just the right time and in just the right way. We immediately complied with his request.

During the question and answer period, Brian attempted to articulate what made his senior pastor's actions so abusive. It was a topic he had never explored. He explained that his senior pastor's harsh words and actions were like blows received in a boxing ring. Brian had tried to shrug them off and minimize their effect, but in reality the mistreatment caused painful wounds to develop that seemed to undermine his manhood. Also, being told by his senior pastor that filling the soda machine would be "his altar alone" caused him to question his calling and effectiveness. The words came with a cruel look and sarcastic tone. Questions rose in Brian's mind. Was God punishing him for some forgotten sin? Brian felt guilty and responsible even though he was convinced he had done nothing wrong.

Even now, Brian had a difficult time thinking of his senior pastor as the source of his emotional wound. He had been taught from childhood that priests are good, safe people who love and serve God. His senior pastor's actions had been malicious and calculated. Brian sensed that he was bleeding emotionally, but felt powerless to stop it.

His wife and family also felt the sting of senior pastor mistreatment. The senior pastor made them feel incompetent and inadequate. He judged, maligned, and demeaned them before others. His attacks, however, were subtle. The senior pastor was careful to stay within the bounds of his office and position. His negative remarks, spoken under the guise of advice or fatherly teaching, made them all the more hurtful and insidious. For a long time, Brian and his family wondered if the senior pastor's comments might be true. Maybe the entire family was lacking and at fault. Introspection sapped their joy and caused them to doubt God and one another. Furthermore, Brian labored under the guilt of feeling responsible, he was sure the attacks were in retaliation for trying to play the senior pastor's game.

Mistreatment toward Brian and his family continued over the course of many months. During this time, Brian experienced what he called "layers of pain." His wounding experiences accumulated and ran together, which seemed to intensify their negative effect. Eventually, he could not remember a time when he felt happy. During these days, it was easy to lapse into self-pity. His mind would drift back to how much he and his family had invested. Their reward for all the sacrifice was sadness, confusion, self-doubt, and loneliness. Brian recounted that during these days he was unable to pray or even think clearly about the painful events. After being dismissed from the church, it was two years before he could face the situation and analyze what had occurred.

The group concluded that one of the most severe blows occurred during Brian's talk with his bishop. Making an appointment with a higher-ranking official was his last resort. He felt that he had done all he could to address his problems. He knew this was a risky thing to do, and that going over the head of a senior pastor was rare and frowned upon. Brian did not want to seem like a stool pigeon. Still, he felt it was worth the risk for the sake of his family and others who might be suffering. He figured that being ignored was his worst-case scenario, and that was exactly what happened. He felt like a fool for confiding in the bishop. He wondered again if all his self-doubts were, in fact, true. Maybe the pain was simply his imagination or his fault. He knew that when word of his visit to the bishop got back to the senior pastor there would be hell to pay. Shortly thereafter Brian was terminated. He felt betrayed by the senior pastor, the bishop, and the religious system he had loved and respected all his life.

It was impossible for group participants not to be affected by Brian's words. Everyone was personally impacted; some cried and others were angry. Surprisingly, however, the dominant emotion was confusion. The group asked questions like, "how could this happen?" and "where is God in all this?" There were no easy answers. Each participant could empathize with how Brian felt. The painful looks on their faces showed that many of them had trust injuries that were still open and raw.

It was clear that recounting these painful events was difficult for Brian, too. He thought he had recovered, but his reaction showed he had not. His words were laced with profanity making it clear that he was still angry and hurt. He wished, knowing what he knows now, that he could go back and stand up against the abusive man who masqueraded as God's representative. Brian was especially frustrated that the wounding senior pastor "got away with" implementing his cruel agenda and he wondered how justice could be served now, so long after the fact. Furthermore, he wondered how he could forgive a senior pastor who had so blatantly wounded his family. He felt that the man deserved to be whipped, not forgiven. But would God judge his lack of forgiveness? How could he forgive when there was no forgiveness in his heart? Admonitions to forgive for the sake of Christ seemed to fall short. Participants felt it unfair of others to make victims feel guilty for not wanting to forgive their victimizers. However, all agreed that they wanted to forgive, they just did not know how.

In assessing the situation, the group agreed that Brian had been mistreated by his senior pastor, and that the pastor had used the influence, power, and prestige of his spiritual office to strip Brian of his manhood, dignity, and calling. The group condemned these actions as demeaning and malicious. The fact that the wounding was done in the church made it all the more painful. The group concluded that addressing senior pastor mistreatment is especially hard because it involves taking on the system itself, which is difficult because the system allows senior pastors to legitimize and spiritualize their harmful actions. In Brian's case, the system was more than willing to allow the senior pastor to maintain the status quo, even though it meant wounding people in the process.

Wendy's Story

I am Wendy, Brian's wife, and this is my story. Nothing in our years of marriage, living and working in the secular arena, or three years of seminary life prepared me for that first church staff position. Brian and I expected our assignment to be as warm, alive, and exhilarating as our seminary life had been. My husband and I knew we had a call from God. The position seemed like a wonderful opportunity for us to grow spiritually and serve a large church family. Our first meeting with the senior pastor was very encouraging. He seemed kind and gracious. I was especially impressed when he assured me that the interior of our house would be painted in the colors of my choice. Most importantly, Brian seemed very happy in his new role.

To find ourselves serving a parish was a joyous milestone of God's grace. We were looking forward to settling in, being invited to people's homes, and inviting them into our home. Our children were happy too. They began exploring the neighborhood and meeting children and families that lived nearby. Our youngest child, six years old, constantly disappeared through the hedge to visit the widow who lived next door. They delighted in each others company. They spent time watching birds, examining flowers, and sampling ice cream together in the cool of the evening. She became my son's adopted grandmother.

Our first Christmas season was full of parties and festivities. I remember standing next to the senior pastor at a party the week before final ordination and asking him the difference between an ordained priest and a deacon. He responded that being ordained a priest allowed a person to be in charge. This conversation would come back to haunt me in later months. For the present, I was excited about my husband's ordination and the fact that our children were to present the elements of bread and wine at Communion.

Ordination day was thrilling. Our children sat with their grandparents to witness the bestowing of Holy Orders. I felt overjoyed and humbled to find myself actually walking down the aisle with my husband, after having invested our lives in the call to service. It was hard to believe that this day had finally arrived. I rejoiced and thanked God. The future looked bright.

Sometime after his ordination, my husband's attitude coming home from church activities began to change. The senior pastor assigned him some new duties that were pretty menial. The tasks didn't bother him, but they took his time away from serving people. We joked about it, but in time more disturbing things started to happen. The senior pastor's tension with us seemed to mount every day. He was critical of my kids and of me, and Brian's ministry opportunities were reduced dramatically.

Eventually, the senior pastor told us that our next door neighbor was being excommunicated and that we must have nothing to do with her. How could he expect us to do that? This was our adopted grandmother. We knew from personal experience that she was a wonderful and godly woman. I decided to investigate and discovered that when her husband died, the senior pastor asked her to donate the property adjacent to the church. Her refusal made him angry, and we were told that they had not spoken since the encounter. It was clear that the excommunication was his way of exacting vengeance. We were enraged, but felt powerless to act. We could not prove anything, and church policy required that such matters be left in the senior pastor's hands.

Tension grew between our family and the senior pastor. Brian tried to talk to him about the growing animosity, but he dismissed it as pettiness on our part. As problems mounted, Brian's frustrations began to be vented toward the family. It was hard for all of us to keep balance. Just when we thought things could not get worse, they did.

One day as our oldest son entered the church garage to use the lawn mower and was angrily accosted by the gardener. He accused our son of snooping and told him to leave. The gardener said that he had spoken with the senior pastor, who told him not to trust the boy. We found ourselves growing emotionally and spiritually impoverished by the senior pastor's hostile actions and attitudes. Even my youngest child was affected. She began to experience breathing problems. The doctor said the problems were due to stress.

After a few months, a secretary finally told us the source of the senior pastor's hostility. She explained that whenever a deacon was ordained to the office of pastor, the senior pastor felt he was in danger of being replaced. His response was to discredit the person or drive him or her out of the ministry. Therefore, it was no surprise when a few months later the senior pastor announced that Brian's contract would not be renewed. On the first of June his salary ended and we were forced to move.

We grieved having to leave our church family. We had formed strong friendships, but now we felt like a boat set adrift. Our kids were angry too. Our two youngest children loved to walk the two blocks from our house to the shops on the corner. One day I came home to find an array of new stuffed toys in the living room. I discovered that they had not been paid for, they had been tucked under coats and brought home by our children. A professional counselor told us that our kids took the toys as a way of acting out their anger. We all cried. The next day we took our kids to face the shop owner. The owner was grateful to them for confessing, but asked them not to come into the store again. The kids were embarrassed and we felt responsible. The stress of our situation had finally caught up with us all.

After we moved, I found it hard to talk about what had happened, and harder still to keep things in perspective. It was all just too painful. I felt rejected, isolated, and cut off. I wanted support, but was reluctant to reach out. I felt like I had to be strong for everyone, which caused me to suppress my feelings. Acting positive exhausted me. I worked hard to appear normal on the outside, but I could do nothing about how I felt on the inside. I knew God was real, but I could not understand why He felt so far away, and I wondered if anger and resentment hindered my prayers.

Group Discussion

Wendy articulated her story with precision and passion. The actual events had occurred years before, but the pain she felt was still vivid. Wendy and Brian's time at seminary had been a rich and wonderful experience. They were led to believe that full-time ministry would be equally fulfilling. Their hopes and expectations were running high as they began their first ministry assignment.

The abusive treatment they received at the hands of their senior pastor was heartbreaking. All they wanted to do was serve, but they were hindered and beat down at every turn. It was especially difficult for Wendy to watch the senior pastor act unkindly toward her children. However, openly confronting him was out of the question. Their level of stress began to rise exponentially.

Their senior pastor's mistreatment caused agonizing questions to trouble their minds. Wendy wondered why God had sent them to this church. The whole family wondered what they had done to deserve such treatment. The senior pastor never communicated anything openly and clearly, instead he joked or spoke sarcastically. The closeness their whole family felt to God diminished as their stress and confusion grew. Family fights and disagreements increased during this time which added to their overall feeling of isolation and despondence. Wendy and Brian began to question God's character and their call to ministry.

As Wendy shared, emotion poured from her. She still felt pain for what her family went through and resentment toward the senior pastor who almost ruined their lives. She thought she had forgiven him, but could not be sure in light of the anger she was feeling. Her spirit still felt fractured.

Wendy thanked everyone for the opportunity to get how she felt "off her chest." She communicated surprise that so much anger and frustration remained after so long a time.

The group speculated that this was due in part to the fact that she was never afforded the chance to talk about what had happened. Before leaving the church she had entertained the idea of talking to the senior pastor, but feared that he would retaliate and cause more problems. Lack of closure caused her to relive the tragic events again and again in her mind. However, at the end of the session, she felt that she had realized a degree of closure.

Asked if she would have done anything differently, Wendy responded that she wished she would have researched the church and senior pastor more carefully before accepting the assignment. Looking back she confessed that she had been naive. At the time she just assumed that all senior pastors were "safe" people worthy of trust. It was a mistake she would never make again.

As she said this, sadness filled the room. Everyone suddenly realized that all had experienced innocence lost. They found themselves longing for the days when they were naïve, passionate, and idealistic. The thought of stolen innocence caused everyone to feel cheated. They cursed the injustice of being wounded by people representing God. All they wanted to do was love and serve, but for their efforts they were cut to pieces.

Kevin's Story

For over three years I volunteered as a children's church director. During this time I became close friends with the senior pastor. When my wife and I had marriage problems, he counseled us. He was always there when we needed him. We told him all our secrets.

Our church was growing rapidly. It felt like God's hand was upon everything we did. The emphasis at church was on quality relationships, close-knit and genuine. One evening my wife and I were in a small group with four couples including the pastor. He told me that I had been hired as the children's church minister. I cried. This was my official acceptance as a full-time salaried staff member.

In no time at all, I settled into my staff role. I loved teaching kids and enjoyed the team that surrounded me. One night, my wife and I went out to dinner with a team member and her husband to celebrate the team member's birthday. During dinner, I discovered that she was an artist. Being a former art teacher, I offered to look at her work. We set a time to meet at my studio.

The session was enjoyable and productive. We found ourselves painting late into the night. After a time, her husband called. I asked if he was concerned about the lateness of the hour. She replied, "he knows how I feel about you." I asked her what she meant. She told me that she had romantic feelings for me. This surprised me and touched a chord deep inside. I hungered to be adored and put on a pedestal. There was nothing physical between us, but as time went on our relationship grew.

During this time, my wife and I grew apart. I was sad about this, but the new relationship made me feel like I had hit the jackpot. Because there was no physical contact, I convinced myself that nothing was wrong. However, one night my wife and I had a huge fight and I went to the house of my new "girlfriend." I spent the night there. The next morning after her husband left for work, I gave her a thank you hug. She said the hug hadn't lasted long enough, so we continued to hug. I attempted to kiss her, but she turned away. After that, we talked for awhile, and then I left.

I spent the next couple nights sleeping in my office. I felt guilty and remorseful. Soon, the team member's husband called the senior pastor and everything came out in the open. I was relieved. I broke down in tears and repented of everything I had done. The next day I was asked to step down as children's church minister.

Up to this point I felt that my senior pastor had acted properly. He confronted me and I willing repented of my sin. In fact, I was glad that the hidden relationship was brought to light. I had been wrong and I knew it. I had to address my inner need to be adored. I was looking forward to being healed with the help of my trusted senior pastor, but soon everything unraveled.

At the next meeting with my senior pastor boss, I noticed a significant change in his attitude. He was sorely disappointed that I hadn't "come clean" earlier. He no longer seemed interested in my healing. Instead, he seemed intent upon making an example of me. He said that if he punished me strongly enough, other men in the congregation would think twice about transgressing as I did.

To punish me, he forbade me from selling my artwork anywhere in the community. He informed a number of Christian businesses and churches in the area that I was a sinner under discipline. Even though I expected to be removed from my staff position, I did not expect to be blackballed. The senior pastor seemed impervious to how his treatment would affect us financially. Furthermore, the public nature of my firing tested our friendships and embarrassed my family. When the senior pastor turned against us, others were afraid not to follow his example. Virtually our entire emotional and spiritual support system evaporated instantly. The senior pastor told us that our only recourse was to submit to his discipline.

After a time, I told him of our financial distress. He agreed to give me a four-month contract as janitor. I didn't mind the work, but it was hard to sense people staring at me. I brought up the awkwardness of the arrangement, but was told to keep looking at my sin.

Discipline was not just directed toward me, it was also aimed at my wife. During previous counseling sessions, the senior pastor had accumulated a lot of information about her. He used this information to brand her a bad wife, mother, and Christian. Specifically, he let it be known that my transgression was mostly her fault. He claimed that her issues would have driven any man away. My wife was devastated. Not only had she been victimized by my indiscretion, she was now being maligned by the one person who had previously been her primary spiritual support. The unfolding of these events also deeply wounded our two children. They felt horrible about how we were being treated. They also felt the pain of being shunned and looked down upon.

After a few months we felt it necessary to leave the church. We really did not want to leave. We wanted to stay and work things out. However, we felt that staying would result in the destruction of our family and our faith. Upon leaving the church, we were excommunicated. People were told to treat us as if we were dead. In many ways we were dead. I doubt if we will ever become fully alive again.

Group Discussion

After Kevin finished sharing, he sat quietly still. It seemed as if he was waiting for us to yell at him, condemning his lapse of judgment. During the testimony he constantly demeaned himself, referring often to "his sin." Six years had gone by since his confession, and it was clear he could still not move forward. His pastor had not forgiven him, and thus, he could not forgive himself. He was locked in a tragic unforgiven state in which he was both sinner and sinned against.

Kevin was especially hurt by the fact that for years prior to the incident, the senior pastor had expressed his undying love and commitment to him and his family. They had all felt completely and unconditionally accepted. At the time, the pastor's love was just what the family needed. However, remembering the love and acceptance of earlier days only intensified their pain of being rejected. They all felt betrayed. It was devastating to realize that the senior pastor cared more about appearances and religious standards than he did about them. Because of this, they began to question the sincerity and love of God. Maybe Christianity itself was nothing more than a cruel cosmic joke.

Apart from being very hurt, Kevin told the group how confused he had felt following the incident. His tears of repentance had been genuine. At first the senior pastor seemed understanding. Kevin was sincerely looking forward to a time of restitution and reconciliation. He knew it would be hard to restore what was lost, but he believed that God would forgive, heal, and redeem. The events that followed shocked him and shook his confidence.

Shortly after his prayer of repentance, Kevin was told that he would be punished "until he was sufficiently sorry." He was also informed that since he had been a staff member an example would have to be made of him. Others would fear as they watched him suffer. Kevin was compared with Esau, who sold his birthright for a bowl of soup. Consequently, he had no rights and deserved no blessing. Kevin had never heard such doctrine before. He asked for a second opinion but was told that the senior pastor alone was the final authority. The fact that the church was large and prosperous made the senior pastor's position even more imposing. Kevin felt helpless. He only had two choices. He could stay in the church and submit to cruel treatment or leave. He and his family chose to leave.

The senior pastor was furious when Kevin informed him of his decision to withdraw from the church. It seemed clear that the senior pastor was only interested in using Kevin's situation as a means to further elevate his status as a leader, healer, and miracle worker. In leaving, the senior pastor likened Kevin to King Saul who was disobedient to the Lord. This devastated Kevin and left him feeling ashamed and guilty. However, even after all he had been through, he was uncomfortable with any thought that his former boss had acted in a malicious and self-centered manner. He wondered if such comments invited God's judgment. The group comforted Kevin and themselves with the thought that God would not punish people for telling the truth.

Linda's Story

My feelings of loss and loneliness connected with Kevin's indiscretion and firing were almost indescribable. I felt abandoned by my husband and the church. Everyone withdrew from me and embraced the other woman. She was protected while I was blamed and disgraced.

To punish my husband for disloyalty, he was given a low-paying position and told that seeking outside work as a Christian artist would invite consequences. After he was fired, we were afraid we wouldn't be able to pay our bills. I felt shunned by the church and abused by the senior pastor. He made me feel like everything was my fault. He told me that if I had been a better wife, this situation would not have happened. Our entire family felt embarrassed. When I tried to share my frustrations with the senior pastor, he accused me of being rebellious. He told me to examine my sins and submit to his decisions. I desperately wanted our family to remain in fellowship but none of us could bear it. I was desperate for a kind word, especially from the women, but was told to repent of what I had done to cause my husband's failure.

I was afraid to submit to the senior pastor, because I felt I was being unfairly measured and judged. Because of his hard stance against us, people in the church who might have wanted to reach out were afraid to do so. In this, the most difficult situation of our lives, we felt orphaned. It's been years, and it is still hard for me to trust Christians because of that feeling.

Just recently the church leadership, my husband, and I all apologized to each other for what happened. However, I still feel like an amputated limb. I long to be made whole again. I still feel a great deal of despair and agony. I continue to cry out to God for restoration and healing.

Group Discussion

Linda and her husband Kevin had invested years serving their ministry and their senior pastor. She poured

114

herself out-behind the scenes loving and serving all who came to her. They both learned how to make do with little money. Even though her husband was a talented and respected teacher and artist, she was content to have him labor in the relative obscurity of church ministry. Serving on a team with loving and committed people was worth that sacrifice. Her entire family felt proud to be part of something alive and worthwhile.

Linda cried as she told her story. Everything had seemed fine until her husband "fell off the pedestal." Staff members were expected to perform to a higher standard. Personal problems or mistakes were not tolerated. When Kevin slipped into the inappropriate emotional relationship, Linda was devastated. She knew their marriage needed work, so she reached out to the senior pastor for help. Instead of help, she received rejection, condemnation, and discipline. Her beloved senior pastor indicted her for her husband's indiscretion.

Linda confided to the group that she never would have believed a church leader capable of such judgmentalism. She lamented the loss of her dreams. She had hoped her children would grow up in the church, marry within the church, and serve God through the church. She had always viewed her church family as permanent. She saw giving to the church as an investment in her own future. She felt that her family had a permanent share in the good things that were sure to come.

When they were forced to leave, Linda felt numb. Over time hopelessness turned to rage as she remembered how much she had invested. Rage turned to anguish as she reflected on how much had been lost. Her life felt like a nightmare. Now, after talking things out, she was beginning to feel hopeful that God might be able to restore what was lost.

Martin's Story

I felt we had come home. This was the church I had always hoped to find. My wife and kids said the same thing. The music was upbeat, Jesus was honored, and people were friendly. The senior pastor and his co-pastor wife were wonderful. They were talented, passionate, and best of all, they loved us. They made us feel special. They took time to get to know us. We willingly opened ourselves to them. We told them our hopes and dreams. We told them our problems and struggles. Together we shared victories and defeats alike. They discovered our gifts and invited us into their ministerial family.

I joined the pastoral staff primarily because I had never before felt such love and acceptance. I worked hard for the ministry and gave large monetary donations when appeals were made. It was a privilege to serve God with such loving and gifted people. My family and I felt secure and safe, loved to the end, no matter what. These were the happiest days of my life, until things started to change.

The changes occurred slowly and subtly over a period of time. One by one the staff started leaving. I thought it was God moving them to other assignments. Everyone who left was careful not to say anything negative or give indication as to the nature of the difficulty. There was just a feeling that something might be very wrong. After a while, problems became more noticeable. The name of Jesus was seldom used in church and Bible references became scarce. Also, Christian terminology was removed from worship songs. When I inquired, I was told that the church was moving toward a more culture-friendly format.

Other changes were more personal but equally disturbing. During a leader's meeting, the pastor's wife misunderstood me to say that I had not finished a staff assignment. The next day she called me into her office to say how disappointed she was with me. When she realized that I had, in fact, completed the assignment she communicated her relief. This disturbed me greatly. I told her that I hoped

116

her care for me was not dependent upon my job performance. I didn't mind being corrected, but I didn't want her
personal disappointment to be used as some kind of
motivational tool. I reminded her that past wounds made the
appearance of withholding acceptance especially disturbing
to me. She made no apology. She said my response to her
statement was something I had to deal with.

Things got worse. While I was away attending
school, my teenage son called to say that the senior pastor
had disciplined him. I called the pastor and asked that any
further communication with my son wait until my return. He
agreed, but later changed his mind and again met with my
son alone. To this day, I do not know what was said in that
meeting. I only know that since that conversation, my son
has been distrustful of spiritual leadership. In going back on
his word, I felt the senior pastor had betrayed my trust. When
I confronted him, he said that he was my spiritual leader and
I had to trust him to do what he thought was right. All this
made me feel uncomfortable and unsafe, but the worst was
yet to come.

A short time later we found out that the youth pastor
was being fired. I did not feel he was being treated fairly, but
I respected the right of the senior pastor to hire and fire. Just
prior to his leaving, I invited the youth leader to come to our
house for a going away party. When the pastor found out, he
told me to cancel my plans. I was shocked. I assured him this
was not a church function, but merely a time to say our
private goodbyes. He would not hear of it. He was convinced
that bad things would be said about the church. I assured him
that in my house nothing like that would be allowed.

He responded by questioning my loyalty and made it
clear that he no longer trusted me. He told me, "It's either
my way or the highway." In an instant I realized that what
had appeared to be genuine love and acceptance for my
family and me was a ploy to get me to join the church and
serve his ministry. Instead of being a loved person, I was just
a ministry tool used to expedite his agenda. The moment I

questioned him, I was dismissed from his mind and heart. His wife followed suit by affirming her husband's decision to shut me and my family out. We felt betrayed, used and abused by people who had promised to love us forever.

It has been five years since my resignation and we still have not found a church to attend. When we do go to church, we usually come home feeling depressed and angry. We have noticed that our comments about church have become laced with cynicism. We still long for the "good old days" when we felt loved. Recently my daughter dreamt that Jesus killed her. How much our wounding experience contributed to this mindset is something we may never know.

Group Discussion

Martin's first emotion following his testimony was surprise. He could not believe that so much hurt and anger still remained in him. After all, it had been five years since his wounding experience. Martin's testimony had been laced with profanity. He had trusted, loved, and served his senior pastor. He treated his senior pastor's kids as his own. The senior pastor's battles were his battles. He gave extra time and significant amounts of money to ministry projects. Martin ended by lamenting, "I did all this and in return he threw me out like garbage."

Group participants were perplexed. In the beginning, Martin's senior pastor seemed like "the real deal." So, what happened? Participants theorized that the problems might have started when a "need to grow" mindset took center stage. After this, the Gospel, once held in high esteem, was changed to accommodate the senior pastor's change in priorities. In the minds of some, Martin was sacrificed on the altar of church growth idolatry.

Especially disturbing was the senior pastor's tendency to set himself up as the church's final authority. Such a posture seemed to foster his caustic "my way or the highway" attitude. When Martin disagreed with the pastor, he was only given two choices; back down or leave. The senior pastor obviously did not want to lose Martin as a resource, but he was not willing to relinquish control either. As a result, Martin was considered expendable. He was driven from the church without so much as a goodbye.

Eric's Story

I began to realize that I was feeling discontented with my job. It was a good position and I was doing well. In fact, I was being offered a promotion. Sometime in the middle of that year, however, I strongly felt that God was leading me to quit. So after much prayer, I quit my job and accepted a full-time position at the church I was attending. My duties included, but were not limited to, leading small groups, training small group leaders, church scheduling, overseeing the bulletin and staffing the church's information center. Also, I was part of the interview process that resulted in the hiring of a new children's church director and a fine arts pastor.

Without warning, one of the staff members decided to resign and move back to California. I was unaware of the reasons for her departure, but I did know that her parting was not amicable. The youth pastor's wife and I planned a going away party for her at my house. I had hosted many church parties before, but there was a real heaviness to this one.

Not long after this, the youth pastor and his wife were dismissed from the staff for reasons not publicly stated. The firing caused them to be stuck with many bills. I went to their home to help them pack. While we were packing, the senior pastor called and left a message on the answering machine. He informed them they would be jeopardizing their severance if they met or talked with any church members. We were all aghast at the senior pastor's fearful and mean-spirited tone.

The senior pastor's callous attitude was starting to concern me. Another problem surfaced during a staff leadership retreat. This was supposed to be a restful and spiritually refreshing weekend. Instead, the focus of the weekend involved participating in highly competitive group games. During a staff meeting earlier in the week, the senior pastor was informed that many leaders were not comfortable participating in such games, but the senior pastor mandated that everyone participate in order to "reach beyond their comfort zones."

A few weeks later, the senior pastor asked me to meet with him because he had heard I was having problems with the church. I told him that I did not feel safe meeting with him alone, and wanted someone else in the room. He expressed disbelief that I felt unsafe, but agreed to have one of the deacons attend the meeting. I attended the meeting for the purpose of offering my resignation.

To begin, I stated that I was seeking closure and that my time on staff was over. The senior pastor said he felt I had unresolved issues against him, and that we needed to discuss these issues. I told him that such a discussion would not be profitable. The senior pastor accused me of sinning because of my refusal. Also, he accused me of being influenced by other staff members who had left the church. I told him that I was unaware of any staff member's reasons for leaving.

Finally, the senior pastor asked what I intended to do. I told him that on Sunday I wanted to say goodbye to the staff and thank them for their friendship and support. The senior pastor said that he did not feel I could do this without being negative toward him. He ordered me to leave the building immediately and never set foot on church property again. After the meeting, I visited some good friends and cried.

For almost two years I floated from one church to another. I was looking for a place where there was genuine concern for people, where the pastor truly had a shepherd's heart. My wounding experience made me angry and cynical. I finally found a good church, but even so, I have yet to recover from the experience.

Group Discussion

Initial group discussion centered upon the heavy investment Eric had made in order to be part of the staff. Eric quit his job, in part, so he could achieve his dream of serving the church full-time. He believed that God approved of his decision. He trusted the senior pastor and believed that he would be a valued part of the leadership team. Soon after he started working, he formed deep friendships with other staff members. Eric felt secure and happy with his new life.

When the senior pastor told Eric to leave the church and never return, he lost his entire investment. His staff friendships were disconnected and his trust in his senior pastor was shattered. Worse than that, Eric lost his sense of purpose. He had been a retired businessman starting a new career in ministry. The senior pastor's mistreatment caused him to become a retired businessman with no sense of direction. He also lost many of his church friendships forged over a long period of time. It was bad enough to be dismissed from the staff, but being dismissed from the church was almost more than he could bear.

The most telling part of Eric's testimony occurred when he told the group that he went to a friend's house and cried. I thought his tears were the result of having been emotionally wounded, and that this wound caused him to go into a type of shock. This reaction seemed to occur the moment Eric realized that a large part of his life, as he had known it only moments before, was now over. The experience filled Eric with a sense of catastrophic loss and grief. He felt numb. It was many weeks before he was able to feel again.

Eric told the group that rage later developed in his heart when he realized that he had been victimized and lied to by the senior pastor. It was devastating to realize that the senior pastor had feigned friendship for the sole purpose of using his gifts and talents. Eric belittled himself for not seeing it coming. Prior to this, he felt that he had been a good judge of character. He was taken aback by his inability to recognize the senior pastor's tactics. Also, he felt confused as to why God had not warned him of the impending dangers. Group participants found it difficult to comment. These were feelings, thoughts, and questions that remained unanswered for them as well.

The participants in our session observed that the senior pastor's definition of loyalty was warped. To him, loyalty was a requirement instead of a gift. The senior pastor defined loyalty as obedience to his every wish. Anyone saying "no" was considered disloyal. Eric lamented that he had always wanted to give the senior pastor his loyalty. But when the senior pastor demanded it rather than asking for it, all of his joy was lost. Eric stated that in any case, he could never be loyal to a senior pastor who used his power and position to mistreat people rather than serve them.

Allison's Story

An evil act changed my life forever. A senior pastor whom I respected and admired ripped away my innocence and ability to trust. One night, at the request of my senior pastor boss, I went to the church office for a meeting. I had no reason to suspect that anything bad would happen; this was my beloved pastor. He was respected in the community and put on a pedestal by many, including my own family. What happened that night thrust me into a living nightmare which still plagues me today.

My senior pastor came into the room and approached me from behind. He touched me and uttered something sexually explicit. It was as though I physically left my body and was observing this scene from above. I watched as my trusted pastor, employer, and father figure raped me. At one point the phone rang. It was his wife. He stood there with his pants around his ankles and his hand over my mouth calmly talking to his wife as though nothing unusual was happening. Ironically, after the act was over, he walked me to my car to ensure my safety. He told me that he would see me at church the next morning.

I drove home in a daze. I was blinded by tears and flooded with feelings of despair. I could never tell anyone what had happened. I knew that no one would believe me. I remember driving onto a bridge and turning my steering wheel hard to the right, hoping I would end up dead at the bottom of the lake. I woke up two hours later, in the hospital, disappointed that my life had been spared. I cried so hard that I promised I would never allow myself to feel again. For the longest time, I would not let anyone near me. I did not want to be touched. I turned away from my friends, fearing I could trust no one.

To this day I ask myself, "Why me, why was I chosen?" I had not asked for this. I had not tempted my perpetrator. Why me God? Why did you let this happen? I still deal with fear and anger. A lot of the anger is directed toward my mom. She idolizes and respects the man who raped me. I have never been able to tell mom and dad what really happened. They would never believe him capable of such a thing. I could tell no one at church for the same reason.

My fears have taken many forms. Initially, I had panic attacks. I was afraid of bosses and men in power. I am still afraid of trusting people. Also, I feared going to a counselor, because I felt that a counselor might not understand. He or she might blame me for what happened. I am still afraid someone will think that what happened was my fault. Today, the perpetrator is on staff at a large church in my area. I know there have been other victims. He needs help and he needs to be stopped before he claims another victim.

Please, parents, listen to your children. Listen to them even when they are saying something impossible to believe. Talk to them when they start acting differently. It is possible they have a terrible tale to tell. There are things about that night I have not told anyone. Shame and the fear of not being believed are still too intense. I know that what happened has affected my marriage. I project a lot of anger toward my husband. I do not think I will ever recover from the horror of what happened. It has ruined my life.

Group Discussion

After hearing Allison's testimony, group participants sat in stunned silence. Initial comments centered upon the depravity and pure evil of the deed. Sadly, participants acknowledged that this was not the first time they had heard of such a thing happening. The group was astonished to hear that the perpetrator was still serving in a paid church leadership position. Most wondered why the pastor was not in jail. Participants commented that Allison had not just been victimized, she had been targeted by an evil person masquerading as a man of God.

As discussion continued, participants speculated as to what factors contributed to this wounding event. Participants observed that the senior pastor had entrapped Allison. Before the encounter, he was careful to make himself a valued family friend. He portrayed himself as a wise father figure worthy of trust. In all likelihood, he hired Allison so he could have access to her at his convenience. Also, he developed a close working relationship with her so her guard would be down. He scripted events in such a way that she would have no way of guessing what was to come. Participants observed that only a very sick person would do such a thing.

It is my opinion that members of Allison's church contributed to this miscarriage of justice. Apparently, some congregational members had heard troubling reports about the senior pastor but chose to ignore them. Congregants may have done this, in part, because they could not bring themselves to believe that the accusations against their pastor might be true. Individually and collectively they seemed unable to face the possibility that this man was evil. It was easier for them not to ask questions then it was to risk making waves. They may have considered it essential to believe the best of their pastor rather than the worst. Also, it is possible members were afraid to speak against "God's anointed."

Participants took a moment to speculate as to Allison's husband's pain. All agreed that the husband must be experiencing significant emotional trauma. Allison, at one point, was concerned that her husband might be tempted to kill her attacker. Participants agreed that the pain resulting from this kind of mistreatment goes far beyond the experience of the victim. It also damages families and can negatively impact future generations.

Reflections

Upon completion of all the testimonies and group discussion, participants took time to reflect on what had been accomplished. Without question visiting the pain of the past had been difficult; however, participants felt they had learned a great deal. They took note of the fact that they shared many symptoms in common, including anger, grief, confusion, a sense of loss, and a diminished sense of self-worth. The emotional pain felt by all had often caused sleeplessness and even nightmares. Additionally, all of the group participants confessed to being confused by their wounding experiences. It was hard to sort out what went wrong. Some found it easier to fault themselves than blame their senior pastor boss. One individual fantasized a scenario where what he had lost was reclaimed. He actually tried to re-insert himself back into the unhealthy church situation until family members and a group participant convinced him of the folly of this action.

Not only had the group participants gained perspective and knowledge, they also found meeting together to be therapeutic. It was a great relief for everyone to get what happened out into the open. Every story was told with emotion. Some of the participants, men and women alike, wept as they recounted the pain of their past. All were deeply appreciative of the fact that each person understood, at least in-part, what the other had experienced, because all had suffered at the hands of their senior pastor and all were abandoned by church systems they thought to be trustworthy. The hugs and kind words shared after each meeting were passionate and filled with love. They penetrated deep into each heart, helping to cleanse and heal. Individual participants ministered the comfort of Christ to their fellows out of the reservoir of their own pain. It was clear that Jesus was in the midst speaking, touching, and comforting.

During the ten week period earnest prayers had been lifted up. I use the word "earnest" not to comment on the group's relative spirituality, but to describe how intensely the need was felt. The collective sense was that if a healing miracle were going to occur, it could only be accomplished by God's hand alone. And at the end of their experience, it was clear that God had shown Himself faithful.

Eric disclosed that Jesus had caused him to realize that he had done all he could to promote peace in the midst of his situation. The Spirit of God directed him to look back on written communication that proved to his heart that he had, indeed, done his best. This helped free Eric from the hurt of the past and helped him take positive steps forward. He felt God motivating him to reach out and socialize with people again instead of just staying at home. Brian added that during the sessions he was motivated to review his pain and find strength in God. Martin was thankful for caring people who loved him and were willing to pray for him. It was God's strength through them that would continue to give him the courage to move forward. Martin also thanked God for breakthroughs concerning family love and unity. He shared that God had used the pain to draw them closer together.

Linda was blessed by those who were able to articulate and confirm her thoughts and feelings. Cleansing occurred as truth was illuminated. Forgiveness and healing no longer seemed impossible. She felt that God was with her as she pressed through the pain and embraced life. Allison knew it was the Spirit enabling her to keep her sanity and live life one day at a time. She felt the hand of God as her marriage continued to grow and flourish.

The ten week session ended with everyone tired but encouraged. It was as if each one had experienced a kind of deliverance, a purging that left one empty but cleansed. Individually and collectively, faith was again being restored that recovery could happen. People felt better about themselves and life in general. Everyone had the expectation that God would continue the good work He had begun. They decided that some time in the future they would again meet together to discuss how God was continuing to work in their lives.

Postscript

Some weeks later the group participants gathered to discuss how God was continuing to heal their lives. Laughter, hugs, and joyous chitchat filled the room as people arrived. Everyone was glad to be together again. It was good to see the joy that shone on each face. How different from the look and sound of days gone-by. Wendy recounted that she awoke one morning with words flowing through her head. She said, "I recognized a narrative going on of the events from that time of wounding in my life. The amazing thing to me is that the pain I expected wasn't there. I could look back on the whole thing objectively. That is God's blessing."

Kevin and Linda's marriage seemed stronger than ever. They were talking more and working out problems they had kept buried for years. Also, they were in the process of visiting churches again to see if God might direct them to a new church home. Martin's life had changed dramatically. The anger that had been so apparent was melting away. After being a critic of the structured church for so long, God was now directing him to help start a church. He was excited that God was showing him how to help the new church stay focused on Christ. He was thrilled to again be part of a church family. Eric, too, had found a new church home. He was teaching a Bible class and mentoring three young men. Eric was happier and more open with people than he had been for years. It was evident he felt much more vibrant and alive.

Allison was also experiencing the healing touch of God. Jesus miraculously opened doors for her family to move into a new home. She was thankful for this new beginning. Also, God opened a door for her to become more active in the community. Allowing the group to hear her story had been a courageous step. It seemed clear that taking this step had somehow opened a channel of bravery in her from which she would always be able to draw.

When group participants rose to say good-bye, they again hugged and expressed thanks for all they meant to each other. They had experienced things no one should ever have to suffer. But through it all Jesus had shown Himself faithful, granting perspective and healing. All were grateful for the realization that what others had meant for evil, God was redeeming and using for their good.

Chapter Seven
Wisdom in the Midst of Madness

Assessing a Leader's Wounding Potential

Senior pastor mistreatment is a contradiction in terms. Church leaders are mandated to love and serve, not wound or damage. However, armed with their own brand of justification, wounding senior pastors devastate lives and place blame for the devastation upon those they wound. When this happens, instead of church being a house of prayer it seems more like a house of madness. Staff associates who work in the church under a senior pastor must keep their eyes open, lest they be overtaken by mistreatment masquerading as ministry. One way to determine whether senior pastors have wounding potential is to examine the gospel they preach.

When the angel announced Christ's birth to the shepherds, he told them that His arrival was "good news" (Lk. 2:10). When Jesus began His ministry, He told the crowds that He was proclaiming the good news of God's Kingdom (Lk. 4:43). The good news Jesus proclaimed was better than anyone could have ever dreamed. He declared the good news of God's love for all people.

The good news of the kingdom involves salvation from death and the promise of eternal life. This gift of God is free, bought and paid for by the blood of Jesus. The gift is not deserved, and it cannot be earned. It can only be received. Indeed, salvation means turning one's life over to Christ, but when Christians give up their lives to Him, He in return shows them how to live. Real life means loving God and serving people.

The good news declares that fear is gone. Every day is lived under the mantle of His grace. The goodness of His table is beyond expectation (Ps. 23:5). He guides steps, conforms people to His image, forgives sins, provides for needs, and so much more. None of this is accomplished through self-effort or works. On the contrary, Christians are instructed to "work hard" to rest (Heb. 4:1-11).

The "good news," however, is not the only gospel being preached today. Many well-meaning senior pastors have wounding potential because they proclaim a "bad news" gospel that emphasizes performance, self-effort, and the need to maintain a legalistic religious standard. This gospel does not rest in what God has done for man; it emphasizes what man must do to be accepted by God. Such a gospel wounds people because it requires that they measure up to an unreachable standard. Those who preach a "bad news" gospel are constantly exhorting people to work harder so they can get to a place where God can use them. When failure occurs, individuals are judged as resisting God or branded as "unsavable." When a bad news gospel of performance is preached, church ceases to be a safe place. Instead of a healing center, it becomes a house of horrors.

RuthAnn, a staff intern, eloquently described the anguish of working for such an organization. After high school, she enrolled in a nationally recognized church leadership program. While she was there, she continually felt judged. Leaders made her feel unworthy and unacceptable. She confided, "They kept telling me that I needed to change and become a different person. I felt that if I didn't conform, Jesus and everyone else would be disappointed in me."[214] This was all very frustrating for her until she realized that all she needed to do was trust God to mold her into the person He wanted her to be. "I accepted the fact that I am too weak to be a 'perfect' Christian, and so is everyone else. I was filled with joy when I realized that Jesus loves me just the way I am."[215] It is true that obedience is a requisite part of what it means to cooperate with God. As C.S. Lewis writes, "Now, the demand was simply 'all.'"[216] But it is God's job to conform us to His image and lead us into His will. RuthAnn's story had a happy ending because she had the courage and wisdom to embrace the one true Gospel.

Survival Skills

Toxic churches led by pastors who preach a bad news gospel are a reality. This will be the case until the healing good news gospel of God completely drowns out the noise of its performance-oriented counterpart. For this to happen, the spiritual paradigm of loving God and serving people must take precedence over corporate mindsets. Until this occurs, staff associates who work in toxic church environments can implement six survival skills that will help them avoid trouble.

1. Do not accept abusive treatment as normal.
   Resist cruelty, coercion, threat, inequity,
   constraint, and competition.

2. Recognize wounding agents for who they are.
   They are self-centered bullies who use sexual,
   physical, verbal, or psychological strategies
   to get what they want.

3. Be alert to being "set up."
   Do not let senior pastors indoctrinate or
   psychologically coerce you into compliance.

4. Seek out a lateral support system.
   If you are being mistreated, chances are you are
   not alone. Ignore the "don't talk" rule and share
   your experiences with others. Wounding senior
   pastors can sometimes be stopped if they are
   confronted by a unified group.

5. Watch your heart.
   Do not give into self-pity, rage, or a judgmental
   attitude. Jesus calls us to pray and look to Him.
   He works all things for good.

6. Don't stay too long.
   It is never God's will for you to remain in a
   wounding church. Exit as soon as possible and
   tell people why you are leaving.

Where to Begin if You've been Wounded

Resolving and recovering from situations of abuse within the church is always difficult. Before healing on anybody's part can happen, all of the parties involved should recognize a few truths that will help the process. First, senior pastors are at fault for the pain and suffering they perpetuate upon their staff employees, and religious organizations are culpable for allowing these abuses to occur. Perpetrators and complicit individuals must be held accountable. At the very least, this accountability should include repentance and some form of restitution. Make no mistake, God is on the side of wounded associates as they cry out for help. However, it must be kept in mind that the goal is not vengeance, but healing. And for healing to happen the need for perspective cannot be overstated.

Perspective requires us to understand that all have sinned and fallen short of God's glory. At some time or other all of us have acted unjustly and must accept the responsibility of repenting and begging forgiveness. Also, perspective acknowledges that although God is on the side of the wounded, He loves perpetrator and victim alike. This is a difficult concept, because victims naturally view perpetrators as being bad people who deserve a horrible judgment against them. Although this may be true, the heart of the law is mercy and God's grace to us all is unmerited. Consequently, God's desire is always that love and compassion carry the day. Wounding senior pastors and their victims share in common the need to experience and feel God's unconditional love. Love is the fertile ground from which faith and good works grow. God's love reminds us that His grace and care extends to all concerned. It is in the arms of Jesus that wounding agents and wounded associates alike can find hope and healing.

Obviously, the quest for perspective is not for the faint of heart. Wounded staff employees must realize that wounding senior pastors are probably not bad through and through. In fact, more often than not, wounding senior

132

pastors injure associates out of their own woundedness. Many of the wounds senior pastors experience come courtesy of corporate-minded religious systems that wound them in the name of promoting ministerial success or securing organizational survival.

Paul, a young spiritually-minded senior pastor, was serving a small congregation in the Midwest when, during a board meeting, he was informed that his salary was going to be placed on a sliding scale. He found out later that this was done to retaliate against a sermon series he had preached a few weeks earlier. The series on repentance apparently hit too close to home for a few families. They informed the board that they would leave if such sermons were ever preached again. The board, fearing financial loss, put Paul's salary on a sliding scale as a warning that any financial fallout would come out of his pocket. Paul was hurt and angry. Over time he became distrustful and suspicious of people. He began to question the motives of his staff. Without realizing it, he began to look out for his own interests. He was sure no one else would.

Paul's story is not uncommon. Many senior pastors are wounded by powerful congregants or church boards that attempt to manipulate policy through intimidation. The potential for such wounding increases exponentially if finances or attendance begin to decrease. When a church becomes anxious about its survival, groups within the church grasp for power in hopes of protecting their interests. Unholy alliances rise up against the senior pastor in the name of protecting the Lord's work. Voices proclaim that pastors come and go, but "we remain the same." Such a battle cry usually culminates in dismissing the senior pastor and bringing in "fresh blood."

Horror stories such as these in no way excuse the abuses that pressured senior pastors all too often bring to bear upon staff associates. Senior pastors have an obligation to stay true to the spiritual paradigm. When their ministry mindset ceases to be about loving God and serving people, especially staff, all is lost. However, these stories are important, because telling them can provide perspective, which is key to the healing process.

I consider perspective to be so important because I have truly seen all of the angles of senior pastor mistreatment. In the introduction to this book, I told a story in which I was wounded by the senior pastor above me. That wounding is, in part, why I feel it important to tell the stories of other abused associates. Along with recovery for mistreated associates, I know there is also hope for wounding senior pastors. I know because God restored me. Take my word for it; wounding agents are hurting and miserable. They are driven by personal demons to control people for their own purposes. Like so many wounding senior pastors, I wounded people out of my own woundedness. Further-more, I did not realize I was doing anything wrong until God opened my eyes.

A number of years ago, I was the senior pastor of a church in Nebraska. One afternoon I thought I would drop in on a leadership conference hosted by a church across town. I do not remember what the speaker said, but I do remember that I felt as if God was speaking directly to me. God pointed out that my heart was not right before Him. I had thought this for some time but had dismissed it. He told me that my thoughts, motivations, and actions were self-centered and not focused on Him or others. At that moment, I realized I had been trying to "make things happen" so that I could look good. I realized that I desperately wanted my supervisors and God to approve of me and be impressed with me. Consequently, I preached a performance-oriented gospel, told people what God wanted them to do, forced compliance, and monitored lives. I unknowingly lied when I told people that I was doing all this for their benefit.

After God opened my heart, I began a long healing journey which culminated in my falling into the loving, affirming, and forgiving arms of Jesus. I slowly began to see that His love for me is unconditional. He loves me for who I

134

am, not for what I can do. Because of what God spoke to my heart, I did a lot of repenting; especially to my family who bore the brunt of my harmful actions. I am so grateful that even though I was a wounding agent, Jesus never gave up on me. He never stopped loving me even though I was resisting Him and hurting others.

If Reconciliation is Your Goal

Occasionally, after wounding has occurred, injured associates turn to a board member, elder, or teacher in the church for help in being reconciled with their senior leader. Such a goal is a worthy pursuit, but should be entered into with extreme caution. This is because reconciliation in matters of abuse in the church is rarely simple. Reconciliation occurs when sinner and sinned against are relationally restored, but achieving true reconciliation can be very difficult if the people doing the wounding have no idea that what they were doing was sinning against fellow Christians. To make matters even more difficult, individuals who seek repentance from their abuser might be hurt so deeply that they do not feel good about forgiving the individual, even if he or she repents. This is all horribly complex and difficult to resolve in a manner that all those involved find satisfying, even among Christians whose common goal is to serve God.

One of the biggest problems with reconciliation in the church is when the people in charge of facilitation favor a philosophy that loses sight of the person and sees ministry as merely mechanistic problem solving. In the same way that corporate-minded churches become more focused on turning a profit than the spiritual health of their members, a mechanistic ministry philosophy replaces relational openness and spiritual sensitivity with scripted answers that are forced into place. Such a philosophy views people and their problems as an equation that must be solved. In such an environment, wounded people and their complaints become integers, points, and relations that are added, measured, and reduced. Mechanistic ministry fails because its foundation is

135

neither spiritual nor organic. Rather, it utilizes a paradigm of linear humanism that seeks to repair broken people by analyzing, arranging, and adding together the sum of their various parts.

The problem with reducing ministry to a series of equations and linear ideas that are meant to apply to all situations is that God is not an equation, He is Spirit. And man is not a machine, but a living being filled with the breath of God. Consequently, men and women are not built to run like watches, they are meant to grow like plants (Ps. 1:3). They are not mechanical things that can be figured out and fixed, but living souls that must be tended and nurtured. Mechanistic ministry is toxic because it works against the true nature of both man and the Spirit. Tragically, it is implemented in most churches as the philosophy of choice where reconciliation is concerned.

For example, the scripted equation used by mechanistic ministries typically includes the mandate that those sinned against forgive their perpetrator "no matter what." The wounded are told that failure to forgive invites God's wrath or hinders His healing touch. Francis, a church worker, experienced an attempt at reconciliation through this mechanistic model. In the course of her duties she had been wounded by her senior leader. Hurt and confused, she took the matter to the church. The elders told her that "no matter what" it was her duty to forgive the pastor and continue serving so God could reconcile them. The elders did not ask how she felt or inquire as to what God might be saying. Instead, they looked at her as a mathematical variable and determined her "value" within the equation. The results were disastrous.

As Francis' story illustrates, any ministry method that requires a scripted one-sided response from the wounded individual, without giving consideration to the wounding agent's need to humbly asses his or her behavior is unfair and unsafe. It is unsafe because it fails to take into consideration the leavening nature and damaging effect of sin. By this I mean that when a person is sinned against, sin's effects penetrate and wound that soul. Moreover, sin's negative effects can spread. For example, what begins as a broken heart can lead to a distorted self-image, which in turn can result in a person becoming depressed.

Mistreated staff associates have been sinned against by senior pastors who have betrayed their trust. Sin is not mechanical, theoretical, or abstract. One way or another, sin always involves harm done to others. It undermines wellness, diminishes self-esteem, and fractures livelihood. When mechanistic ministry mandates that the sinned against reconcile with a wounding agent without first addressing the harm done to them, it rewards the perpetrator with "cheap grace" and encourages him or her to keep on sinning. Such ministry is ungracious and unjust because it offers grace and restored relationship to the sinner without considering the needs of the sinned against. This conveys the idea that justice-making is irrelevant. In contrast, Holy Spirit-directed ministry is relational and organic. The sinned against are allowed to speak. They are heard, respected, and taken seriously. They offer prayer and receive wisdom as to how growth and healing can be expedited.

Under this spiritual paradigm, reconciliation begins when the seeds of repentance and restitution are planted together with the wounded person's seed of forgiveness. These seeds contain the Spirit's DNA. They are alive with the very nature, character, and presence of God. There is nothing mechanical about how these seeds grow. They cannot be plugged in, added up, or arranged together to produce a pre-determined crop of choice. These seeds grow according to God's will, drawing sinner and sinned against together. Over time, these plantings mature to become healing grapes of gladness from which drips love's sweet wine (Amo. 9:13). Sinner and sinned against drink deeply of this mixture. It restores the fortunes of weary souls and rebuilds the ruin of relationships lost (9:14). The fragrance of this sweet wine rises to Heaven's throne. God inhabits this

137

offering and pours out a blessing that cannot be contained. This blessing changes the scarlet color of sin to purest white. It turns sadness into uproarious laughter, and does away with the worst kind of evil for the good of all concerned. It restores trust and community unity out of which flows the blessing of God (Ps. 133).

However, much of the time wounding senior pastors fail to participate in this process. They refuse to acknowledge even the possibility of wrongdoing. Such denial makes genuine reconciliation virtually impossible. Furthermore, this denial makes it difficult for wounded staff associates to grant forgiveness; difficult but not impossible.

Forgiveness: A Plausible Definition

Each time I have experienced wounding at the hands of a senior leader, forgiveness has been a huge issue for me. On each occasion (there were two), the last thing I wanted to do was forgive. Well-meaning people told me of my need to forgive, but I was skeptical. I knew that withholding forgiveness would not keep me out of Heaven or alter God's love for me because Ephesians 2:8-9 tells me I am saved by grace through faith, not by any ability I may or may not have to successfully grant forgiveness. Furthermore, there was the problem of needing to be truthful. God values truth and sincerity (Ps. 51:6), and in all honesty, I did not feel there was forgiveness in my heart to give away. Any attempt to utter the words "I forgive" in any context would have been hypocritical at best.

Theological issues aside, the real problem for me was twofold. First, my anger made me feel guilty. Whether I had reason to feel this way or not was irrelevant to the point. Second, I wanted to be able to extend grace if for no other reason than wanting to move beyond my pain. However, my hurt and anger made this impossible. It was in the midst of feeling frozen in place that I went to God and asked myself in His presence, if there was anything good in my heart that I could "in truth" give away. Funny as it sounds, at that

138

moment the only good I could extend was not slashing his tires and dumping trash on his lawn. Even though it didn't seem like much, it was all my heart had to give. Even this, I felt, was more than he deserved.

After I made this transaction before God a wonderful and surprising thing happened. I felt better, a lot better. I felt peaceful and even "righteous" in the best sense of the word; not self-approved, but clean. It seems, the moment I extended the good I had in my heart, I began to freely breathe again, even live again. It dawned on me that in not slashing his tires or throwing trash on his lawn, I was in fact extending forgiveness. I think the problem is that as Christians, we have been taught a very narrow and idealized definition of forgiveness. We have been told that forgiving means forgetting, letting go, and having nothing but good feelings. To me, however, this is more like what it means to be reconciled, which requires repentance and restitution on the part of the offending party. On the other hand, it seems to me that a proper understanding of forgiveness has its root in Hebrews 12:14, which reads, "Try to live in peace with all people" (International Children's Bible). Living in peace in no way obligates Christians to forget, let go, or have good feelings. It does not necessarily mean going to the person involved; however, it does involve extending truthfully and without pretense, whatever "good" happens to be in one's heart. How this good manifests itself is of little consequence. The point is that a person can only give what is in their possession. If God puts more good in their heart at a later date, so be it. But until that time, individuals who have extended what forgiveness they can are free to be at peace in the situation knowing they truly tried to follow God, and in doing so, fulfilled all righteousness.

Fulfilling Righteousness

On the occasion of Christ's baptism, John the Baptist protested that he should be baptized by Christ, not the other way around. Even though John's point was well taken, Jesus asked John to baptize Him so that "all righteousness" might be fulfilled (Matt. 3:15). By doing this, Jesus abandoned His rights and humbled Himself to show forth the lengths to which God would go to make mankind righteous again. In like manner, wounded staff associates fulfill all righteousness when they extend whatever they can that is good toward those who have hurt them. It fulfills all righteousness because it selflessly extends the unmerited grace and mercy of God.

Another example of fulfilling all righteousness in the Bible occurs when Jesus pardons his persecutors from the cross (Lk. 23:34). In forgiving His killers, Jesus exhibits a righteousness that is as judgmental as it is gracious. Jesus judges what is being done to Him as sin, yet graciously forgives. Such righteousness "only makes sense within the story of a God whose judgment is gracious, whose will is ever directed toward the mercy that brings new life."[217]

Such is the righteousness wounded staff associates are invited to extend. They first judge what the wounding senior pastor did to them as sin. After this, they rise in all righteousness and announce that the penalty for this sin is God's forgiveness. Such a response rightly calls the wounding a sin and righteously declares the sin to be forgiven because of the blood of Jesus. In this scenario, whatever good a wounded associate can extend becomes a premeditated act of grace-filled retribution. It restores dignity to the sinned against and aids the recovery process because it empowers the victim to simultaneously deliver a blow and extend a grace. Forgiveness as a judgment of grace fulfills all righteousness. However, it in no way obligates the sinned against to feel good about, embrace, restore, or even interact with the wounding agent. That involves reconciliation, or justice-making, which can only occur if perpetrators are willing to humble themselves and prove that their repentance is real (Lk. 3:8).

Epilogue

To everything there is a season. Indeed, someday soon Jesus will return for the bride he loves. When that day comes, senior pastor mistreatment and the resultant trust injuries will be swept away. Until then, we must reach out to wounded senior pastors and staff associates alike. In the arms of Jesus, there is healing and forgiveness for all.

As the church awaits the Lord's return, Her calling is to be faithful (Matt. 24:45-47). This cannot be achieved through a corporate mandate. It can only take root as a spiritual paradigm is embraced. This spiritual paradigm emphasizes loving God and serving people above all else.

Loving God and serving people has always been the prime directive for the church. The apostle Paul tells us in Galatians 5:13-14, "My brothers, God called you to be free. But do not use your freedom as an excuse to do the things that please your sinful self. Serve each other with love. The whole law is made complete in this one command: 'Love your neighbor as you love yourself'" (International Children's Bible). Therefore, with all that is in us, let us give our lives to Him and to one another in loving service. Let us love in such a way that He will be able to commend us for being good and faithful servants (Matt.25:23).

.

END NOTES

[1] Davis, *Allies In Healing,* 13.

[2] Weiser, *Healers: Harmed and Harmful*, 77.

[3] Weiser, *Healers: Harmed & Harmful*, 3.

[4] Powell, "Expected Vocational Roles," 234.

[5] Coulter, *Gospel of Rescue,* 1.

[6] Powell, "Expected Vocational Roles," 234.

[7] Weiser, *Healers: Harmed and Harmful,* 4.

[8] Ibid., 88.

[9] Horney, *Our Inner Conflicts*, 42-43.

[10] Weiser, *Healers: Harmed and Harmful,* 39.

[11] Barna, *Turning Vision Into Action*, 105.

[12] Aubrey Malphurs, "Maintaining the Vision" *Leadership Handbook of Management and Administration*, ed. James D. Berkley (Grand Rapids: Baker Books, 1994), 161.

[13] Powell, "Expected Vocational Roles," 36.

[14] Bixby, "Designing a Church Pastoral Staff."

[15] Sanford, *Ministry Burnout*, 62.

[16] Sanford, *Ministry Burnout,* 31.

[17] C. Peter Wagner, "Leading Versus Enabling," *Leadership Handbook of Management and Administration*, ed. James D Berkley (Grand Rapids: Baker Books, 1994), 152.

[18] Barna, *Power of Vision*, 32.

[19] Ibid., 33.

[20] Ibid., 32-33.

[21] Ibid., 45.

[22] Malphurs, "Maintaining the Vision," 161.

[23] Maxwell, *Developing Leaders*, 49.

[24] Barna, *The Power of Vision,* 48.

[25] Campolo,"The Will to Power."

[26] Donald P. Smith, *Clergy in the Crossfire*, 23.

[27] Goldenson, *Dictionary of Psychology and Psychiatry*, 644.

[28] Powell, "Expected Vocational Roles," 27.

[29] Gleason, "Stress Among Clergy."

[30] Powell, "Expected Vocational Roles," 33.

[31] Ibid., 50.

[32] Malphurs, "Communicating the Vision," 159.

[33] Powell, "Expected Vocational Roles," 31.

[34] Sanford, *Ministry Burnout*, 13.

[35] Ibid., 75.

[36] Easum, "Stress Points in Turnaround Churches."

[37] Ibid.

[38] Sittler, *Grace Notes and Other Fragments*, 59.

[39] Ross, "Preventing an Untimely Resignation."

[40] Greg E. Asimakoupoulos, "A Private and a Public Person," *Leadership Handbook of Management and Administration*, ed. James D. Berkley (Grand Rapids: Baker Books, 1994), 6.

[41] Wicks, *Clinical Handbook of Pasotral Counseling,* 91.

[42] Sanford, *Ministry Burnout,* 6.

[43] Easum, "Stress Points in Turnaround Churches."

[44] Sittler, *Grace Notes,* 63.

[45] Mills and Koval, *Stress in the Ministry.*

[46] Mulder, "Who Pastors the Pastor?" 6.

[47] Edmonson, "It Only Hurts On Monday," 218.

[48] Powell, "Expected Vocational Roles," 53, 54.

[49] Weiser, *Healers: Harmed and Harmful,* 42.

[50] Ibid.

[51] Horney, *New Ways in Psychoanalysis,* 75.

[52] Powell, "Expected Vocational Roles," 242.

[53] Ibid., 241.

[54] Ibid.

[55] "How Pure Must a Pastor Be?"

[56] Sanford, *Ministry Burnout,* 44.

[57] Powell, "Expected Vocational Roles," 242.

[58] Horney, *Neurosis and Human Growth,* 13.

[59] Ibid., 22.

[60] Shupe, Stacey, and Darnell, *Bad Pastors,* 1.

[61] Powell, "Expected Vocational Roles," 236.

[62] Weiser, *Healers: Harmed and Harmful*, 77.

[63] Ibid., 74.

[64] Ibid., 29.

[65] Ibid., 43.

[66] Cook, *Love, Acceptance and Forgiveness*, 13.

[67] Barna, *How to Increase Giving,* 139.

[68] Bergman, "Sociology of Religious Organizations."

[69] Sittler, *Grace Notes,* 59-60.

[70] Campolo, "The Will to Power."

[71] Ibid.

[72] "The Curse of the Revolving Door Pastor."

[73] Fehlauer, "Warning Signs of Spiritual Abuse."

[74] Bergman, "Sociology of Religious Organizations."

[75] Flippo and Watson, "The Children's Pastor."

[76] Campbell, "Without Grace."

[77] *Professional Conduct in Adversity.*

[78] Dresselhaus, "Passing the Torch."

[79] Ibid.

[80] McDonald, "Pastors are from Mars."

[81] Marillo, on-air resignation.

[82] Poling, *Abuse of Power*, 13.

[83] Loomer, "Two Conceptions of Power."

[84] Matthews, "Kill or Be Killed."

[85] Ibid.

[86] McCartney and Holbeche, "Roffey Park Management Agenda." This research sampled 372 managers across all sectors of employment.

[87] Matthews, "Kill or Be Killed."

[88] Poling, The Abuse of Power, 90.

[89] Bixby, "Designing a Pastoral Staff."

[90] Wookey, *When a Church Becomes a Cult,* 43.

[91] "The Curse of the Revolving Door Pastor."

[92] McCabe, "No Yelling From the Stands."

[93] Kennedy, "Cutting-Edge Leadership."

[94] Bonhoeffer, *No Rusty Swords*, 186-200.

[95] Dunnam, *The Manipulator and The Church*, 53.

[96] Powell, "Expected Vocational Roles," 40.

[97] Wookey, *When a Church Becomes a Cult*, 106.

[98] Bernard J.Tyrell, S. J. "Christotherapy: An Approach to Facilitating Psychospiritual Healing and Growth," *Clinical Handbook of Pastoral Counseling*, ed. Robert J. Wicks, Richard D. Parsons, and Donald Capps, (NY: Paulist Press, 1993), 60.

[99] Gregory Fisher, Foursquare East Africa Coordinator, interview by author, June 13, 2003.

[100] Fischer, "Dysfunctional Pastor."

[101] Bixby, "Designing a Pastoral Staff."

[102] Dresselhaus, "Passing the Torch."

[103] Namie and Namie, *Bully at Work*, 76.

[104] Allen, "Lifelong Follower-Leader."

[105] Dunnam, Herbutson, and Shostrom, *Manipulator and the Church,* 72.

[106] Blank, *Natural Laws of Leadership,* 61.

[107] Barna, *Power of Vision,* 141.

[108] Maxwell, *Developing Leaders,* 17.

[109] Wise, "The Boston Church."

[110] Singer, *Cults in our Midst.*

[111] Campbell, "Without Grace."

[112] Fehlauer, "Warning Signs of Spiritual Abuse."

[113] Ray Anderson, *Soul of Ministry,* 192.

[114] "Uncovering Churches that Abuse."

[115] Ibid.

[116] Longman, "Mind Control and Manipulation."

[117] Hanson, "A Healthy Church."
[118] Bergman, "The Sociology of Religious Organizations."

[119] Campbell, "Without Grace."

[120] Dunnam, *The Manipulator and The Church,* 68-69.

[121] "Uncovering Churches that Abuse."

[122] "Aaron's Story."

[123] "Baruch Goldstein's Memories."

[124] Ibid.

[125] Ibid.

[126] Ibid.

[127] "Aaron's Story."

[128] Ibid.

[129] Campbell, "Without Grace."

[130] Hornstein, *Brutal Bosses,* 73.

[131] Fehlauer, "Warning Signs of Spiritual Abuse."

[132] Wise, "The Boston Church."

[133] "Uncovering Churches that Abuse."

[134] Ibid.

[135] Campbell, "Without Grace."

[136] "Aaron's Story."

[137] Zukeran, "Abusive Churches."

[138] Ibid.

[139] "Aaron's Story."

[140] Ibid.

[141] Hornstein, *Brutal Bosses*, 17.

[142] "Baruch Goldstein's Memories."

[143] Ibid.

[144] Fortune, *Is Nothing Sacred*, 24.

[145] Hornstein, *Brutal Bosses*, 73.

[146] "Baruch Goldstein's Memories."

[147] *Report on Torture*, 52.

[148] These stages are summarized from Albert Biderman's "Chart of Coercion" printed in Amnesty International Report on Torture, London: Farror, Straus, and Giroux Gerald Duckworth & Co., 1975, 53.

[149] *Report on Torture*, 50.

[150] Mann, "Psychological Abuse In The Workplace."

[151] Langone, "Deception, Dependency and Dread."

[152] Ibid.

[153] Langone, "Deception, Dependency and Dread."

[154] Ibid.

[155] Ibid.

[156] *Report on Torture*, 43.

[157] Ibid., 49.

[158] Zukeran, "Abusive Churches."

[159] Mann, "Psychological Abuse in the Workplace."

[160] *Report on Torture,* 39-40.

[161] Ibid., 51.

[162] Maxwell, *Born Crucified*, 127.

[163] Pinkham, Waters, and Woodson, *Identity Formation*, 17.

[164] *The New Strong's Exhaustive Concordance of the Bible,* "Greek Dictionary of the New Testament," #26, 7.

[165] Lawrenz and Green, *Overcoming Grief and Trauma,* 31-32.

[166] *Diagnostic and Statistical Manual on Mental Disorders: **Dsm-IV**,* 485.

[167] Bloom, *Creating Sanctuary,* 49.

[168] Coulter, "A Gospel of Rescue," 19.

[169] Ibid., 29.

[170] *Diagnostic and Statistical Manual on Mental Disorders: **Dsm-IV**,* 424-425.

[171] Coulter, "A Gospel of Rescue," 32.

[172] Pinkham, Waters, and Woodson, *Identity Formation,* 15.

[173] Ibid., 46.

[174] Mitchell and Anderson, *All Our Losses All Our Griefs,* 36.

[175] Ibid., 26.

[176] Ibid., 45.

[177] Ibid., 64.

[178] Hornstein, *Brutal Bosses,* X.

[179] Mitchell and Anderson, *All Our Losses All Our Griefs,* 37-38.

[180] Milligan, "What I've Learned about Spiritual Abuse."

[181] Mitchell and Anderson, *All Our Losses All Our Griefs,* 50.

[182] Weiser, *Healers: Harmed & Harmful,* 100.

[183] Mitchell and Anderson, *All Our Losses All Our Griefs,* 79.

[184] Lewis, *A Grief Observed*, 27.

[185] DeBlassie, *Toxic Christianity*, 27.

[186] Ibid., 28.

[187] Mitchell and Anderson, *All Our Losses All Our Griefs*, 40.

[188] Ibid., 40.

[189] Sittler, *Grace Notes*, 25.

[190] Anderson, *Soul of Ministry*, 208.

[191] Mitchell and Anderson, *All Our Losses All Our Griefs*, 43.

[192] Doug Glynn, interview by author, 12 February 2003.

[193] Leith Anderson, "Volunteer Recruitment," *Leadership Handbook of Management and Administration*, ed. James D. Berkley (Grand Rapids: Baker Books, 1994), 277.

[194] Julie L. Bloss, "Job Descriptions," *Leadership Handbook of Management and Administration*, ed. James D. Berkley (Grand Rapids: Baker Books, 1994), 223.

[195] Ibid., 223.

[196] DeBlassie, *Toxic Christianity*, 146.

[197] Mitchell and Anderson, *All Our Losses All Our Griefs*, 54.

[198] Bowlby, *Attachment and Loss*, 208.

[199] Mitchell and Anderson, *All Our Losses All Our Griefs*, 28.

[200] Ibid., 61.

[201] Milligan, "What I've Learned about Spiritual Abuse."

[202] Mitchell and Anderson, *All Our Losses All Our Griefs*, 88.

[203] Yeats, "A Deep-Sworn Vow."

[204] Weiser, *Healers: Harmed &Harmful,* 100.

[205] Ibid., 145.

[206] Ibid., 27.

[207] Wipf, "Tough Transitions."

[208] Namie and Namie, *Bully at Work,* 272-276.

[209] Milligan, "What I've Learned About Spiritual Abuse."

[210] Park, *The Other Side of Sin*, 165-178.

[211] *Professional Conduct in Adversity.*

[212] Rentz, "How to Kill a Youth Ministry."

[213] Coulter, "A Gospel of Rescue," 103-105.

[214] RuthAnn Setser, interview by author, Spring 2004.

[215] Ibid.

[216] Lewis, *Surprised by Joy*, 228.

[217] Jones, *Embracing Forgiveness*, 97.

BIBLIOGRAPHY

"Aaron's Story: 'Put to Death Therefore What Is Earthly in You.'" *Ex-Jews for Jesus.* http://www.exjewsforjesus.org/stories/aaron.html (accessed 15 September 2003).

Allen, Gary R. "The Minister As A Lifelong Follower-Leader." *Enrichment Journal* (Spring 2002). http://enrichmentjournal.ag.org/200202/200202_038_follow_leader.cfm (accessed 23 January 2003).

Anderson, Ray S. *The Soul of Ministry.* Louisville: Westminster John Knox Press, 1997.

Banks, Robert J. *Paul's Idea of Community.* Peabody, MA: Peabody-Hendrickson, 1994.

Barna, George. *How to Increase Giving in Your Church.* Ventura: Regal Books, 1997.

Barna, George. *Power of Vision.* Ventura: Regal Books, 1984.

Barna, George. *Turning Vision Into Action.* Ventura: Regal Books, 1996.

Barrett, Donna L. "Matters of the Heart." *Enrichment Journal* (Fall 1998). http://enrichmentjournal.ag.org/199804/090_matters_heart.cfm (accessed January 23, 2003).

Barton, Judith S. ed., *Comprehensive Bureau of Applied Social Research.* Columbia University, 1970.

"Baruch Goldstein's Memories of Jews for Jesus and Moishe Rosen." *Ex Jews for Jesus.* http://www.exjewsforjesus.org/stories/baruch2.html (accessed 19 June 2003).

Bergman, Jerry. "The Sociology of Religious Organizations." *The American Scientific Affiliation* (June 1987). http://www.asa3.org/ASA/PSCF/1987/PSCF6-87Bergman.html (accessed 15 June 2003).

Berkley, James D., ed. *Leadership Handbook of Management and Administration.* Grand Rapids: Baker Books, 1994.

Biehler, Robert. *Psychology Applied to Teaching.* Boston: Houghton Mifflin Company, 1978.

Bixby, Howard L. "Designing a Church Pastoral Staff." *Journal of Ministry and Theology* (1.1 1997). http://www.bbc.edu/journal/volume1_1/designing_staff-bixby.pdf (accessed 20 March 2003).

Blank, Warren. *Natural Laws of Leadership.* NY: Amacom Pub., 1995.

Bloom, Sandra. *Creating Sanctuary, Toward the Evolution of Sane Societies.* NY: Routledge 1997.

Blue, Ken. *Authority to Heal.* Downers Grove, IL: Intervarsity Press, 1987.

Bonhoeffer, Dietrich. *No Rusty Swords.* NY: Harper and Row, 1965.

Bowlby, John. *Attachment and loss*: Volume I – Attachment. NY: Basic Books, 1969.

Brown, Daniel A. *Enjoying Your Journey with God*. Lake Mary: Strang Communications Company, 2001.

Brown, Daniel A. "Help, My Church Won't Grow." *Ministry Today*, July/August, 2003.

Brown, Daniel A. *The Other Side of Pastoral Ministry: Using Process Leadership to Transform Your Church*. Grand Rapids: Zondervan Publishing, 1995.

Bussell, Harrold. *Unholy Devotion*. Grand Rapids: Zondervan, 1983.

Campbell, Michelle. "Without Grace: The Story of Michelle Campbell." *Triumphing Over London Cults*. http://www.tolc.org/campbell.htm (accessed 22 March 2003).

Campolo, Tony. "The Will to Power." Youth Worker Journal. *http://www.youthspecialties.com/articles/topics/staff_relatio nships/will_power.php* (accessed 29 June 2003).

Clinton, Robert J. *Making of a Leader*. Colorado Springs: NavPress, 1988.

Coggins, C. C. "Toward a Definition of Individual Growth in the Rural Community Problem Solving Context." Ph. D. diss, University of Wisconsin, 1976.

Combs, Arthur W. and Donald Snygg. *Individual Behavior, A New Frame of Reference for Psychology*. N.Y. Harper and Row, 1959.

Cook, Jerry. *Love, Acceptance and Forgiveness*. Ventura: Regal Books, 1979.

Coulter, Leah. "A Gospel of Rescue and Relationship for the Sinned Against." Ph. D. diss, Fuller Theological Seminary, 2001.

"The Curse of the Revolving-Door Pastor." *Youth Specialities* (2000). http://www.youthspecialties.com/articles/topics/staff_relatio nships/revolving_door.php (15 August 2003).

Davis, Laura. *Allies In Healing*. New York: Harper Perennial, 1991.

DeBlassie III, Paul. *Toxic Christianity*. NY: Crossroad Publishing, 1992.

Diagnostic and Statistical Manual on Mental Disorders: Dsm-IV, 4th ed. Washington, D.C. : American Psychiatric Publishing, Inc., 1994.

Dobbins, Dr. Richard. "Are You Fit To Be Tied . . . or Fit To Serve? Staying Emotionally Healthy in the Ministry." *Enrichment Journal (Summer 2002)*. *http://enrichmentjournal.ag.org/200203/200203_032_health ypastor.cfm* (accessed 15 September 2003).

Dresselhaus, Dr. Richard L. "Passing the Torch: The Art of Mentoring Staff." *Enrichment Journal* (Winter 2003). http://enrichmentjournal.ag.org/ 200301/200301_066_passingtorch.cfm (accessed 8 August 2003).

Dunnam, Maxie D., Gary J. Herbertson, and Everett L. Shostrom. *The Manipulator and The Church*. NY: Abingdon Press, 1968.

Easum, William. "How to Address the Stress Points in Turnaround Churches." *EBA* (June 2001). http://www.easumbandy.com/resources/index.php?action=details&record=358 (accessed10 August 2003).

Edmonson, Robert L. "It Only Hurts On Monday." D.Min. diss, Talbot School of Theology, 1995.

Ellison, Craig W. and William S. Matilla. "The Needs of Evangelical Leaders in the United States." *Journal of Psychology and Theology*, vol. 11, (Spring 1983): 28-32.

Fehlauer, Mike. "Warning Signs of Spiritual Abuse." CBN.com. http://cbn.org/spirituallife/churchandministry/Spiritual_Abuse1.asp (accessed 10 August 2003).

Fischer, Mark F. "Dysfunctional Pastor, Dysfunctional Council." *Today's Parish* (September 1994). http://users.adelphia.net/~markfischer/A21.htm (accessed 10 August 2003).

Flippo, Lon and J. D. Watson. "The Children's Pastor and the Sr. Pastor." *Enrichment Journal* (Spring, 1999). http://enrichmentjournal.ag.org/199902/104_chd_sr_pastor.cfm (accessed 5 June 2003).

Fortune, Marie. *Is Nothing Sacred?* San Francisco: Harper-San Francisco, 1989.

Frost, Jack. "Why Pastors Fall Into Sin." *MinistriesToday* (March/April 2003).

http://www.ministriestoday.com/a.php?ArticleID=7293 (accessed 23 January 2003).

Gardner, John. "Succession, Challenge and Concerns." Paper presented at the *National Assoc. Evangelical National Conference*, 1988.

Gelles, Richard and Murray Straus. *Intimate Violence*. NY: Simon and Schuster, 1988.

Glaser, Barney G. and Anselm Strauss. *Discovery of Grounded Theory: Strategies for Qualitative Research*. Hawthorne, NY: Aldine de Gruyter, 1967.

Gleason, J. J. "Perceptions of Stress Among Clergy and Their Spouses." *Journal of Pastoral Care*, 31 (1977) 248-251.

Goldenson, Robert M. *Longman Dictionary of Psychology and Psychiatry*. New York: Longman, 1984.

Greenfield, Guy. *The Wounded Minister*. Grand Rapids: Baker Books, 2002.

Guggenbuhl-Craig, Adolf. *Eros on Crutches*. Dallas: Spring Publications, 1980.

Hanegraff, Hendrick H. "The Untouchables." *Christian Research Journal* (Fall 1991). http://www.equip.org/free/DP065.htm (accessed 23 January 2003).

Hanson, Rebecca. "A Healthy Church." *Ex-Cultworld Magazine*. www.caic.org.au/biblebase/abuse/rh_home.htm (accessed 22 March 2003).

Hart, Archibald. "Understanding Burnout." *Theology, News and Notes*, 31, 1 March 1984.

Healey, Robert M. "The Ministerial Mystique." *Christian Century*, February 1974.

Herman, Judith Lewis. *Trauma and Recovery*. NY: Basic Books, 1992.

Herzel, Ron. "The Bible and Spiritual Abuse." *Resources for Recovery*.
http://www.geocities.com/Athens/Forum/9575/biblespirab.html (accessed 1 May 2003).

Horney, Karen. "Finding the Real Self." *American Journal of Psychoanalysis*, 8, 1949.

Horney, Karen. *Neurosis and Human Growth*. NY: W. W. Norton & CO., 1939.

Horney, Karen. *New Ways in Psychoanalysis*. NY: W. W. Norton & CO., 1939.

Horney, Karen. *Self Analysis*. New York: W. W. Norton and & CO., 1970.

Hornstein, *Harvey A. Brutal Bosses*. NY: Riverhead Books, 1996.

"How Pure Must a Pastor Be?" *ChristianityToday.com* Leadership (April 1, 1988). http://www.ctlibrary.com/13487 (accessed 20 January 2003).

Hughes, MaryEllen. "Maintaining the Well-Being of Clergy." Ph.D. diss, Ohio State University, 1988.

Jones, Gregory L. *Embodying Forgiveness*. Grand Rapids: WM. B. Eerdman's, 1995.

Kennedy, Jeff P. "Called to a Cutting-Edge Leadership Strategy." *Enrichment Journal* (Winter 2001). http://enrichmentjournal.ag.org/200101/0101_030_cutting_e dge.cfm (accessed 23 January 2003).

Kriozere , David and Joel Kleinbau. "The Other Side of the Coin." Dovetail, #9:6 July/Aug 2001.

Ladd, George Eldon. *A Theology of the New Testament*. Grand Rapids: Eerdmans, 1993.

Langone, Michael. "Deception, Dependency & Dread." *ICSA*. http://www.csj.org/infoserv_articles/langone_michael_ddd.ht mhtm (accessed18 October 2003).

Langs, Robert J., MD. *The Technique of Psychoanalytic Psychology, Vol. 2*. Jason Aronson, Inc., 1989.

Lattimer, Maxine. "Mass Resignations at SPUC." *Pro+Choice Forum* (7 September 1999). http://www.prochoiceforum.org.uk/comm17.asp (accessed 16 September 2003).

Lawrenz Mel, and Daniel Green, *Overcoming Grief and Trauma (Strategic Pastoral Counseling Resources)*. Grand Rapids: Baker Books, 1996.

Lesser, Charles. "Is Your Church Free From Cultic Tendencies." *Spiritual Counterfeits Project Newsletter*, October 1991.

Lewis, C.S. *A Grief Observed*. San Francisco: Harper-San Francisco, 1961.

Lewis, C.S. *Surprised by Joy*. New York: Harcort Brace and Company, 1955.

Longman Jr. Robert. "Mind Control and Manipulation." *Spirithome.com*. www.spirithome.com/paramind.html (accessed 15 Aug 2002).

Loomer, Bernard. "Two Conceptions of Power." *Religion Online* (10 January 2004). http://www.religion-online.org/showarticle.asp?title=2359 (accessed 10 May 2004).

Mahler, Margaret S. *On Human Symbiosis and the Vicissitudes of Individuation: Infantile Psychosis*. NY: International Universities Press Inc. 1970.

Mann, Robyn. "Psychological Abuse in the Workplace." The University of Adelaide. http://www.adelaide.edu.an/hr/ohs/occstress/psychabuse/biderman.htm (accessed 1 April 2003).

Martin, Paul R. "Dispelling the Myths: The Psychological Consequences of Cultic Involvement." *Christian Research Institute*. http://www.iclnet.org/pub/resources/text/cri/cri-jrnl/web/crj0048a.html (accessed 1 May 2003).

Matthews, Virginia. "Kill or Be Killed." *The Guardian* (27 January 2003). http/www./guardian.com.uk (accessed 20 September 2003).

Maxwell, John C. *Developing the Leaders Around You*. Nashville: Thomas Nelson Pub., 1995.

Maxwell, L. E. *Born Crucified*. Chicago: Moody Bible Press, 1945.

McBurney, Louisa. *Every Pastor Needs a Pastor*. Waco: Word, 1977.

McCabe, Daniel. "No Yelling from the Stands." *Christianity Today* (2001 Winter vol. XXII). http://www.ctlibrary.com/9597 (accessed 15 September 2003).

McCartney, Clare and Linda Holbeche. "Roffey Park Management Agenda." *Roffeypark*. http://www.roffeypark.com/research/index.html (accessed 20 September 2003).

McDonald, Tom. "Pastors are from Mars, Worship Leaders are from Venus." *Enrichment Journal* (Fall 2002). http://enrichmentjournal.ag.org/200204/200204_144_mars.cfm (accessed 12 March 2003).

Melroy, J. "Narcissistic Psychopathology and the Clergy." *Pastoral Psychology*, 35, 1 Fall, 1986.

Milligan, Barbara. "What I've Learned about Spiritual Abuse." *Spiritual Abuse Recovery*. http://spiritualabuse.com/dox/barb.htm (accessed 1 April 2003).

Mills, Edgar W. and John P. Koval. *Stress in the Ministry*. Washington, D.C.: Ministries Board, 1977.

Mitchell, Kenneth, R. Anderson, Herbert. *All Our Losses All Our Griefs*. Philadelphia: The Westminster Press 1983.

Mulder, Edwin. "Who Pastors the Pastor?" *The Church Herald*, 48,7 July, August 1991.

Murillo, Mario A. Transcript of on-air resignation from Wake Up Call on WBAI March 9, 2001 *wbaiaction.org* (3/9/2001). http://wbaiaction.org/statements/01-03-09mmurillo.html (accessed 15 Sept 2003).

Murphy, Jim and Carolyn Murphy. "Exercising Authority." *Hundred Fold Ministries International.* http://www.hundredfold.org/articles/03jan.htmk (accessed 11 Oct 2003).

Namie, Gary and Ruth Namie. *Bully at Work*. Naperville: Sourcebooks Inc., 2000.

Park, Andrew Sung. *The Other Side of Sin*. NY: State University of New York Press, 2001.

Pinkham, Wesley M., Chris Waters, and Sandra Woodson. *Identity Formation: The Journey toward Personhood.* (Manuscript submitted for publication, 2000).

Poling, James Newton. *Power and Abuse of Power*. Nashville: Abingdon Press, 1991.

Powell, Kara Eckmann. "Expected Vocational Roles in the Pastorate; An Experiential Examination and Practical Theology of Intervention." Ph. D. diss, Fuller Theological Seminary, 2001.

Pratt, Benjamin W. "Burnout: A Spiritual Pilgrimage." *Surviving in Ministry*. Ed. Robert R. Lute and Bruce T. Taylor. New Jersey: Paulist Press, 1990.

Professional Conduct in Adversity; A Guide for Church Musicians. Louisville: Presbyterian Assoc. of Musicians (2002). http://www.presbymusic.org/ProfResConduct.htm (accessed 15 September 2003).

Rentz, Eddie V. "How To Kill a Youth Ministry (For Senior Pastors Only.)" *Enrichment Journal* (Winter 2001.) http://www.ag.org/EnrichmentJournal/200101/0101_016_kil l_youthmin.cfm (accesses 15 September 2003).

Report on Torture. Amnesty International. NY: Farrar, Straus, and Giroux, 1975.

Roberts, Ron, and Robert Kloss. *Social Movements*. St. Louis: C.V. Mosby Co., 1979.

Ross, Don E. "Preventing an Untimely Resignation." *Enrichment Journal* (April, 1997). http://enrichmentjournal.ag.org/199704/070_resigtnation.cfm (accessed 13 June 2003).

Sanford, John. *Ministry Burnout*. New York: Paulist Press, 1982.

Schutz, Alfred. *Alfred Schutz on Phenomenology and Social Relations: Selected Writings. ed.* Helmut R. Wagner. Chicago: University of Chicago Press, 1970.

Shelly, Marshall. "The Problems of Battered Pastors." *Christianity Today*, 29, 8 May 17, 1985.

Shupe, Anson, William A. Stacey, and Susan E. Darnell. *Bad Pastors*. New York: New York University Press, 2000.

Singer, Margaret Thayer, with Janja Lalach. *Cults in Our Midst: The Hidden Menace in Our Everyday Lives.* San Francisco: Jossey-Bass Publishers, 1995.

Sittler, Joseph A. *Grace Notes and Other Fragments.* Philadelphia: Fortress Press, 1981.

Smith, Donald P. *Clergy in the Crossfire.* Philadelphia: Westminster Press, 1981.

Smith, Carol. "The Changing Season." *Leadership Journal* (Spring 2000). http://www.ctlibrary.com/le/2000/spring/24.107.html (accessed 15 September 2003).

Smith, Edward M. *Beyond Tolerable Recovery.* Campbellsville, KY: Atlantic, 1996.

Snell, Tim. "Growing in your Relationship with Christ." *Book II Knowing What You Believe.* Appleton, WI: self published, 2000.

Solomon, Charles R. *The Rejection Syndrome.* Wheaton: Tyndale House, 1983.

Sweet, Leonard. *Soul Tsunami.* Grand Rapids: Zondervan, 1999.

Swensen, Richard A. *The Overload Syndrome.* Colorado Springs: NavPress, 1998.

"The Curse of the Revolving Door Pastor." *Youth Worker,* (July/August 1998). http://www.youthspecialties.com/articles/topics/staff_relatio nships/revolving_door.php (accessed 15 August 2003).

Thesaurus of Psychological Index of Terms, 5th Edition.
Washington, D. C.: American Psychological Assoc., 1988.

"Uncovering Churches that Abuse People." *Recovering from Spiritual Abuse* (17 May 1997).
http://www.geocities.com/hotsprings/3658/question.html
(accessed 15 June 2003).

VanVonderen, David and Jeff Johnson. *The Subtle Power of Spiritual Abuse*. Minneapolis: Bethany Press, 1991.

Weiser, Conrad W. *Healers: Harmed & Harmful*.
Minneapolis: Fortress Press, 1994.

Weiss, Daniel S. and Charles R. Marmar. "Impact of Event Scale-Revised." *Victim's Web* (1997).
http://www.swin.edu.au/victims/resources/assessment/ptsd/ies-r.html (accessed 19 July 2004).

White, John and Ken Blue. *Healing the Wounded*. UK: Inter-Varsity Press, 1985.

Whitfield, Dr. Charles. *Memory and Abuse*, Remembering and Healing the Effects of Trauma. Deerfield Beach, Florida: Health Communications, Inc.1995.

Wicks, J. Robert, Richard D. Parsons, and Donald E. Capps, ed. *Clinical Handbook of Pastoral Counseling*. New Jersy: Paulist Press. January 1985.

Wipf, Elaine. "Tough Transitions: When You Have to Leave," *Enrichment Journal* (summer 2002).
http://enrichmentjournal.ag.org/200003/098_tough.transitions.cfm (accessed 12 March 2000).

Wise, Russ. "The Boston Church." *Probe Ministries* (1997). http://www.probe.org/content/view/60/65/ (accessed10 April 2003).

Woley, Dale D. "Spiritual Abuse in the Pulpit and the Pew." *Spiritual Abuse Recovery* 920020. http://spiritualabuse.com/dox/dw.htm (accessed 1 April 2003).

Wookey, Stephen. *When a Church Becomes a Cult*. London: Hodder & Stoughten, Limited, 1996.

Yeats, William Butler. "A Deep Sworn Vow." *PoemHunter*. http://www.poemhunter.com/p/m/poem.asp?poet=3057&poem=45772 (accessed 14 September 2003).

Zukeran, Patrick. "Abusive Churches." *Leadership U* (5 August 2003) http://www.leaderu.com/orgs/probe/docs/abuse-ch.html (accessed 15 October 2003).

Barnabas Group

Barnabas Group is dedicated to coming alongside staff associates who have experienced workplace abuse in the church. If you need help or wish to assist, please e-mail: johnsetser@hotmail.com. For a listing of Barnabas Group services and ministry offerings, visit our website at www.shatteredtrust.com

Made in the USA
Columbia, SC
30 January 2024